The wisdom in rethinking your life!

Copyright © 2012
Revised Edition - August 2015

Published and distributed in the United States by:
Leadership Education Action Programs (LEAP)
2443 Fair Oaks Blvd. #437
Sacramento, CA 95825
800-606-4227
www.wisdominre.org

All the charts and exercises trademarked or copyrighted in this book are the property of CARTE, INC. (Child Abuse Resolved through Education) and Leadership Education Action Programs (LEAP). All rights reserved. No part of this book may be reproduced by any technological, photographic, or mechanical means, or otherwise be copied for private or public use. This book was published to raise funds for the significant work of the nonprofit organization. Net proceeds will fund STARR for Teens (Succeed through Accountable Responsible Resolve) personal development programs for high-risk teen girls and women victims of domestic violence.

RE ©2012 by CARTE, INC. (Child Abuse Resolved through Education), a 501 (c) (3) Nonprofit Organization and Leadership Education Action Programs (LEAP) www.wisdominre.org

TABLE OF CONTENTS

PART 1

Endorsements..06

Introduction..08
    Reflect—Reframe

The Hartman Color Code Personality Profile........................14
    Why You Do What You Do!
    Reassess—Reinterpret

The PIE of Your LIFE 17
    Reevaluate—Recommit

Partner in Excellence (PIE) Testimonies................................22

PART 2

Gloria's Story..26
Coauthor's Journey from Regret and Disappointment
    Reinspire—Reinvent

Rose's Story..37
"In a New York Minute Everything Can Change"
Coauthor's Life-Changing Story of Recovery
    Rethink Everything!

Bobbi's Story..46
    Rediscover—Reaffirm

Sharon's Story..56
    Refocus—Resolve

Sydnee's Story..65
    Re-engage—Rebuild

Nancy's Story......72
Reveal—Restrengthen

Annette's Story......78
Redefine—Restart

Lynne's Story......85
Reconnect—Rekindle

Elizabeth's Story......93
Recapture—Refine

The Heart in Forgiveness......103
Recognize—Respond—Recalibrate

PART 3

A Mindful Me Is a Healthy Me......114
Reclaim—Restore

A Strategic Plan for a Healthier Lifestyle......123
Refuel—Re-energize

Breakdown-Breakthrough......135
Recharge—Renew

Achieving Your Goals and Living Your Dreams......140
Re-story—Recalibrate

ABOUT

CARTE, INC. (Child Abuse Resolved through Education)......146

Leadership Education Action Programs (LEAP)......149

Notes......153

Acknowledgements......159

Authors' Bios......162

PART 1

RE™
The wisdom in rethinking your life!

ENDORSEMENTS

" *RE* demonstrates the significant impact of social-emotional intelligence in understanding our motives and connecting with others. Through the exercises, thought-provoking material, and courageous testimonies the authors have produced a doorway to change and renewal."

- **Dr. Taylor Hartman**
  Founder of *The Hartman Color Code Personality Profile* and author of *The People Code*

" *RE* is an inspirational book to help any woman redefine herself and her relationships in a healthy way."

- **John Gray, Ph.D.**, Author of *Men Are from Mars, Women Are from Venus*

" I first participated in the authors' course called Partner in Excellence (PIE) in Pittsburgh in 2011. It was one of the best choices I have ever made for my personal life and professional career. I use the tools that I learned in PIE every day. As a result, I have taken some giant leaps, achieved big goals, and healed personal relationships. I wish I had been fortunate enough to do the STARR for teens when I was a teenager. *RE*, is an extension of the work the authors have been doing for several years through the personal-growth courses—PIE for women and STARR for teens. The book is a very empowering process you can personally do for yourself from home. I have read through the manuscript and found for me it reinforced the principles and practices from the course. *RE* will transform the lives of many women, teens, and their families."

- **Beth Caldwell** – Founder of Pittsburgh Professional Women, author of three books, *Get Paid What You're Worth*, *I Wish I'd Known That -Secrets to Success in Business from Women Who've Been There*, and *Inspired Entrepreneurs*.

" I am honored to have been the first to read through *RE*, especially since it is designed for women. From a man's viewpoint —I think the book is amazing! Any woman who reads this book, and takes action, will enjoy a healthier and more balanced lifestyle. You have provided the readers with a basic tool to re-story their lives and the exercises will help in mapping out their strategy for success. As you have said in the book, we can't rewrite our past but we can change our response to it. I, too, believe in seizing each moment, and living with passion and abundance. I have been fortunate to have consulted with other authors and experts over the years on sound mind-body philosophy. For me, the book reinforced everything my wife and I have been doing to create more balance in our lives. That can be an enormous challenge with four children. I hope this book is incredibly successful."

- **John Chapman** – Cybris, IT Consultant

" Many years ago I met Gloria Manchester through the seminar company where I started as a basic instructor for personal-growth courses. She was a student and one of the most active enrollers in the business. When she and Rose Gibbons started their own seminar enterprise, Leadership Education Action Programs, they invited me to help them develop and facilitate an advanced personal development curriculum. I had previously participated in working with Dr. John Gray in facilitating their nonprofit STARR SuperCamp for abused teen boys and girls. It was an incredible and powerful experience! These professional women are dedicated to providing quality experiential courses for women and teens, and I wholeheartedly support their work. *RE* is an expansion of their commitment to this worthy calling."

- **Dan Dorr,** Dan Dorr and Associates

" What a powerful and life-changing book! The exercises facilitate self-awareness, reveal self-imposed barriers, and provide opportunities for meaningful growth and change. I was able to face and overcome some of my own professional obstacles after reading the book and completing the exercises. I highly recommend *RE* to both my clients and colleagues."

- **Jan Pollitt,** Licensed Clinical Social Worker, Orange County, CA

INTRODUCTION

At various points in our lives we often re-enact our childhood conditioning or other disappointments and regrets, whether it be from abuse, illness, death, betrayal, divorce, career, or financial loss. Until we consciously recognize how these negative circumstances are limiting us today, and we choose to respond differently, we will not restore and renew our lives.

As women, even in the middle of our busy lives we long to find balance. Though we may continue to set powerful goals for ourselves and start out committed to them ... *shit happens*. There will always be circumstances that will challenge us. It is not what happens to us or what gets in our way that defines us, it is how we perceive and handle what happens. This book is designed to guide and support you in making constructive changes in your life regardless of your circumstances.

RE is a "do-over" guide, a GPS for reinventing ourselves using the same principles and practices offered in the personal-growth and women's leadership courses facilitated by the authors. We all have our stories. Real shift happens when we are willing to do whatever it takes to reclaim our hearts and rewrite those stories. In this book you will be inspired by the intimate testimonies of a few courageous women who made meaningful changes in their own lives using these same principles. SHIFT HAPPENS out of a recommitment to our relationships, career, health, and service to others.

Once we committed to publishing this book, the universe began to test the depth of our own commitment. If we had been circumstance-driven rather than intention-driven in writing *RE*, we probably would have given up early in this process. If we had never moved past the fear of going forward in spite of the circumstances, this project would have never materialized. "Shit Happens" and "Shift Happens," as long as we remain open to all the possibilities. If accomplishing great things in life were easy, each woman would have everything she wants. At the onset of this project, Rose, one of the coauthors, almost died twice, as you will read in her story. We had to rethink everything!

We all have our stories. The story you have been telling yourself has gotten you exactly where you are today. Any negative event in your past that you may be consciously or unconsciously re-enacting need not have been tragic to be limiting you or holding you back. *A cup of pain is a cup of pain.* The courageous women who have told their scars-to-stars stories in this book disclosed the negative re-enactments they have overcome in their own lives, because they wanted to make a difference in your life. *"Scars remind us where we've been, they don't have to dictate where we are going."* (Quote taken from an episode of Criminal Minds)

As any mother who has given birth to more than one child knows, we are born with a specific personality that is intertwined in our DNA. Our unique personality traits and core motives are readily evident at birth regardless of culture, race, or nationality. However, as you will discover later in this book, much of the architecture of our adult brains and neural wiring is shaped by our experiences (filters) in infancy and early childhood. At birth, we have most of the neurons we will ever have, though the connections between our neurons, how they are organized, and communicate with each other are not yet developed.

These connective networks are user-dependent; in other words, they are strengthened, refined, and reinforced by repeated stimulation and experience or pruned and eliminated by a lack of activation or use. From birth to about three years of age, these connective pathways develop rapidly. *As everything is new, there is no other time in our life that is as significant in sculpturing and laying down these communication pathways or neural connections.* It is at this accelerated phase of development that we are downloading the underpinnings of our beliefs, values, perceptions, and attitudes. Our parents and caregivers, then, are instrumental in healthy brain development based on what they do or do not repeatedly expose us to. Everything we smell, taste, hear, see, touch or otherwise experience is embedded in our bodies, hearts and minds.

Though infancy and early childhood are critical for healthy brain growth and development, the brain remains plastic throughout adulthood. It continues to change and is responsive to repeated stimulation, activation, and exposure. It has, in fact, the ability to repair damaged connections by creating new connections. *As adults, then, we have the power to re-story our lives in much larger measure than we once thought possible.*

Interestingly most people experience a very strong urge to think negatively about themselves and the world. This is the human condition. According to Shawn Achor, who was trained at Harvard by some of the pioneers of Positive Psychology, *"we can retrain our brains to spot patterns of possibility, so we can see and seize opportunities wherever we look."* In any given moment, by making the conscious choice to shift your thoughts from the negative to the positive, you can achieve life-changing results.

RE is one such opportunity for you to effectively make constant changes using principles and practices drawn from the authors' own personal and professional experiences, observations while facilitating courses, and from coaching women and teens. And, once you have a clear picture of your unique self-portrait from the comprehensive Hartman Color Code Personality Profile identified in the next few pages, you will not only discover *why you do what you do*, you will also have the consciousness to choose differently. It all begins with you. The decisions you make today will not only impact you, your family, your community, and the world in the present, your decisions will change the course of your future.

Ask yourself these questions: What negative events, regrets, and disappointments am I re-enacting in my life today? And, am I ready for a breakthrough? In order to have a breakthrough, you must be willing to tell yourself the truth and make some meaningful changes. The truth shall set you free! As Rick Warren, pastor and author of *The Purpose Driven Life* says, *"What we reveal we can heal."*

Start now, using *RE* as a GPS to map out your life-changing strategy. It is our hope that no matter what your life circumstances are today, you will seize this moment to make a shift. You can't rewrite your past; however, you can, change your response to it. So, we invite you to join us on this journey to re-story your life.

As you begin to understand your core motives and how they drive your behavior, you are taking the first step in being the **CEO of Achieving Winning Results** in your own life. Looking at the chart on the next page from the bottom up, it starts with your innate personality, your unique DNA. Again, by the time we are three years of age, our repeated experiences and exposures, whether negative or positive, shape brain, mind, and body development, as well as, our perception of ourselves and the world. This is why parenting is such an awesome responsibility!

From these early perceptions we develop certain attitudes that shape our thinking and feeling about ourselves. As an adult we need to get conscious and rethink—do these beliefs, perceptions, and attitudes still work for me? If not, then make a shift in your thinking and make the necessary changes to get you where you want to be today!

"We change our behavior when the pain of staying the same becomes greater than the pain of changing. Consequences give us the pain that motivates us to change."
—Dr. Henry Cloud
Author of *Boundaries*

To paraphrase author and speaker, John Maxwell, there are three main reasons people change:

> They HURT so much they have to change.
> They LEARN so much they want to change.
> They RECEIVE so much they initiate change.

LEAP WINNING RESULTS CHART™

In order to be the CEO of your own life you must bring the following three qualities to the game:

Commitment	Living in commitment is having a clear intention for your life, standing up for your beliefs, saying what you mean and meaning what you say, keeping your agreements, and being willing to shift and recalibrate along the way.
Excellence Vs. Perfectionism	Too often excellence and perfectionism have been used interchangeably. In relationships and in life, excellence is operating at your best with room for flexibility and forgiveness. Perfectionism is a limitation driven by judgment and unrealistic expectations of yourself and others.
Open to Change and Opportunity	*We are either driven by our circumstances or open to change and opportunity.* When you are willing to see the opportunity in everything, you expand your vision. Based on your attitudes you make decisions and choices. The actions you take determine your results.

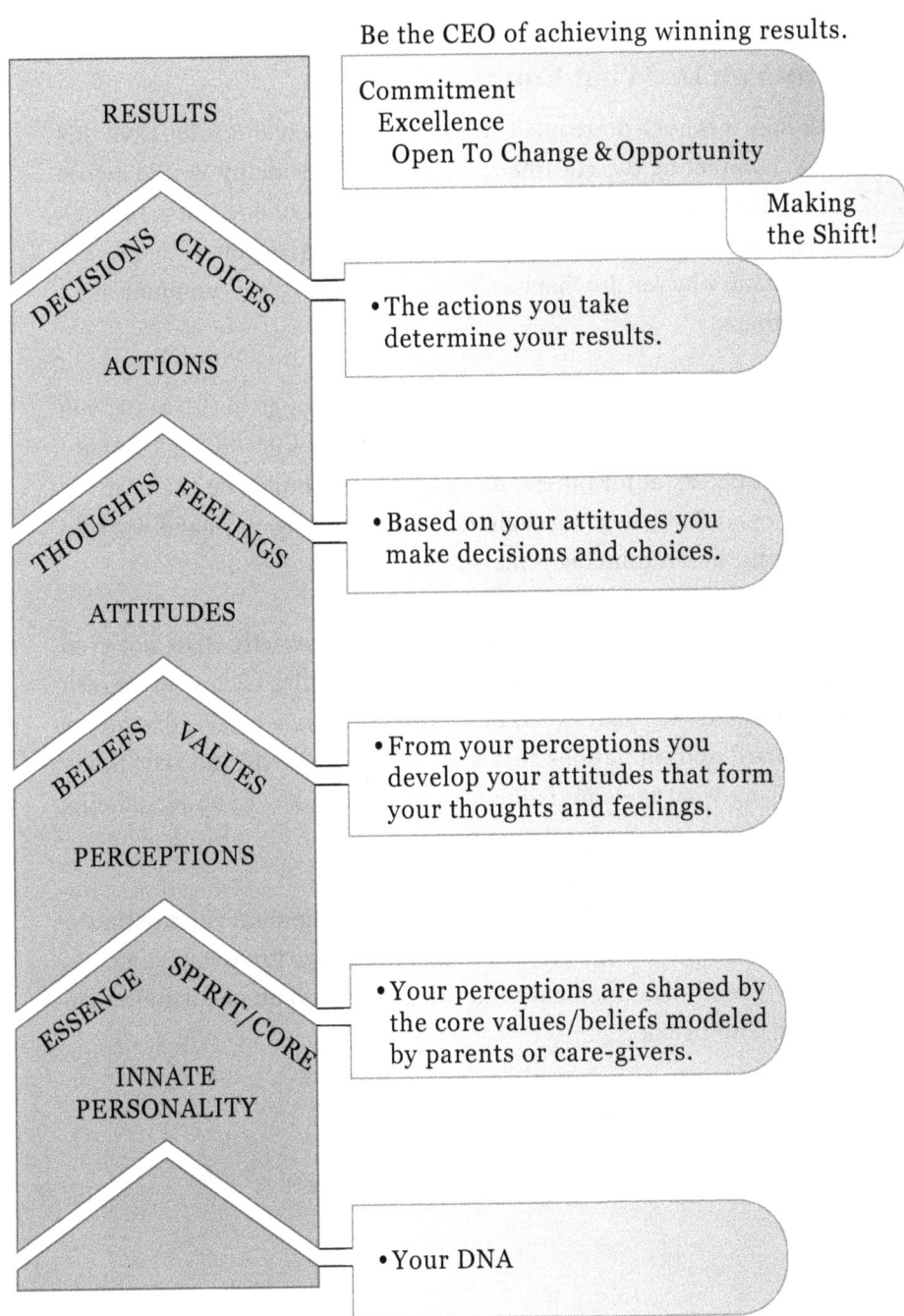

THE HARTMAN COLOR CODE PERSONALITY PROFILE

Why You Do What You Do!

Although it is not a prerequisite for gaining tremendous value from this book, completing the Hartman Color Code Personality Profile before you begin reading will enhance and personalize your navigation through it. This profile identifies your innate color and gives you a blueprint to understand why you do what you do and to improve your communication with others.

Now, as you move through the strategies for change in this book, you can immediately apply the practices and principles in your life that have been so successful for others. As each exercise builds on the next, we recommend that you go through the book reflecting on what is working in your life and rethinking what isn't!

Though we are one-of-a-kind, no two of us are exactly alike, not even identical twins, there are four innate personalities each with its own motive that drives behavior. As individuals we have strengths that propel us forward and limitations that hold us back. Clearly and specifically identifying what they are is the first step and a key to understanding ourselves and effectively relating to others.

To complete the free self-assessment and watch the short video outlining the value of color coding your life, we invite you to go to www.wisdominre.org/colorcode. You must have internet access and an email address to acquire your profile.

Core Motives and Natural Talents

RED — Core Motive: Power
Natural Gifts: Vision and Leadership

Natural Strengths: Action-oriented, determined, decisive, and confident

Natural Limitations: Insensitive, argumentative, critical, and demanding

BLUE — Core Motive: Intimacy
Natural Gifts: Quality and Service

Natural Strengths: Compassionate, thoughtful, committed, and analytical

Natural Limitations: Over-sensitive, perfectionist, worry-prone, and judgmental

WHITE — Core Motive: Peace
Natural Gifts: Clarity and Tolerance

Natural Strengths: Diplomatic, good listener, inventive, and voice of reason

Natural Limitations: Unmotivated, indecisive, silently stubborn, and avoids conflict

YELLOW — Core Motive: Fun
Natural Gifts: Enthusiasm and Optimism

Natural Strengths: Sociable, spontaneous, persuasive, and insightful

Natural Limitations: Poor follow through, impulsive, self-centered, and interrupter

We have only listed a few of the natural strengths and limitations for each color. When upgrading to the full assessment, you will get a comprehensive description of your innate personality, a list of your unique individual strengths and limitations, your typical needs and wants, and a description of the four personality colors. You will also receive an explanation of how your unique experiences filter or impact your self-expression, how to leverage your strengths, and how to character yourself by developing the strengths of other colors. In the Hartman Color Code your driving motive, not your behavior, is the key.

> Personality is a gift. Character is victory!"
> - Dr. Taylor Hartman,
>   Author and creator of *The People Code-It's ALL About your Innate Motive* and *Color your Future-Using the Character Code to Enhance Your Life*

Dr. Hartman means that though we come out of the womb with a specific innate personality (core color) we character ourselves by developing the strengths (positive traits) of our own and the three other colors. When we allow our negative traits (limitations) to hold us back we encounter resistance everywhere in life and conflicts in our relationships. Acknowledging our limitations and recognizing how they affect both us and others around us is essential to growing our emotional intelligence (EI). Our willingness to shift and develop our strengths is the work we all must do to character ourselves and when we do, this is the victory!

The cost of the comprehensive evaluation is $30—the net proceeds go to CARTE, INC. (Child Abuse Resolved through Education) scholarship fund to support under-served women and high-risk teens in participating in accelerated self-esteem programs. Go to www.wisdominre.org/colorcode

---

RE ©2012 BY CARTE, INC. (CHILD ABUSE RESOLVED THROUGH EDUCATION), A 501C3 NONPROFIT ORGANIZATION AND LEADERSHIP EDUCATION ACTION PROGRAMS (LEAP) WWW.WISDOMINRE.ORG

LEAP PIE OF YOUR LIFE™

The eight essential pieces of the PIE of Life are described below and designed to give you a gauge by which to reassess your life today, what's working and what's not working. In a survey done on Oprah with Anthony Robbins, they discovered there is one area in life that women of today seek most to improve: achieving balance. By rating yourself in each of the eight areas you will be determining your starting point. As you read, rate yourself in each category from 1-10, 10 being most in balance and 1 representing there is much work to be done.

1. **Emotional Health** – How do you respond and cope, as opposed to react, to life's circumstances and the world around you? Are you experiencing the balance you want in your life? When stressed, are you over-using food or using alcohol/drugs and other detrimental means to avoid your challenges? Are you recognizing the need to make healthier choices and take responsible action? This need may include confiding in someone you trust, being in a support group, or participating in professional coaching or counseling. Asking for support is an important element in developing yourself. _____

2. **Finances/Career** – Are you earning enough money to take care of your needs and desires? Do you have what you want, are you in a career or job that gives you satisfaction, are you re-budgeting (as it becomes necessary), refreshing yourself through continued learning and educational programs. How often do you recommit to your financial goals (if married, your goals as a couple)?
_____

3. **Marriage/Primary Relationship** – How would you rate yourself in partnership with your significant other? Are you open and honest? Are you communicating your wants/needs and are your needs being met? Are you meeting their needs? Are you being respectful and asking for respect? Are you a good model for other women and for your children? Are you enjoying regular date nights, weekend retreats, 'micro' vacations (those intimate moments or expressions of love and affection)? Do you suggest and set the stage for participation in couples workshops or counseling? How often do you recharge or revitalize your relationship? Do you need to reinvent yourself in your relationship? _____

4. **Family/Other Relationships** – This may include children, parents, siblings, extended family and friends. Are you respectful of yourself and others in relationships? Are you caring, open, and truthful? Do you appreciate the differences in others, their strengths, gifts, talents, and dreams, as well as your children's differences and developmental stages? Do you support others in being the best they can be or do you devalue yourself and others in words or actions. Are you problem-focused or solution-oriented? Do you have realistic or unrealistic expectations of yourself or others? Do you remain self-righteous in your position? Do you often have a need to be right? Do you freely give acknowledgement and encouragement, reassurance, and recognition to yourself and others? _____

5. **Service/Community** – Are you being in contribution to your family and your community or serving in some way in your church, a charity, or nonprofit? How often do you return an act of kindness, pay it forward, or reconnect with your passion and greater purpose? The second most common area women seek to develop (second to balance) is having a sense of purpose and significance.
_____

6. **Spirituality/Prayer/Meditation** – Are you setting aside a quiet time for prayer, meditation, stress relief, and personal reflection? Do you occasionally get massages, facials, or pedicures? On a daily basis, do you give yourself time to rest, relax, reflect, and regenerate? We all need daily bread; it is not weekly or monthly bread. _____

7. **Fun/Recreation** – Are you regularly connecting with family, friends, colleagues in a relaxed or playful atmosphere, and hanging out or playing with kids or grandkids? Are you finding time to indulge in a hobby you love—cooking, gardening, reading, riding a bike, playing a round of golf or tennis, going to a movie, enjoying intimate moments with your significant other, listening to music, soaking in a bath ... whatever may be fun, relaxing, or enjoyable for you? _____

8. **Physical Health** – Are you routinely re-energizing your body—through exercising, healthy eating, drinking enough water, (hydrating and refueling your body), managing your weight, taking proper vitamins and supplements, and getting sufficient sleep? Do you schedule regular doctor visits for various check-ups? If you are taking prescription drugs, are you educating yourself on their effects on your body and mind? According to Adele Davis, nutritionist and author of *Optimum Health*, "The way I see it, every day you do one of two things, build health or produce disease in yourself." Where's your focus? How would you rate yourself in this area?_____

LEAP PIE OF YOUR LIFE™

Rate yourself from 1-10, 10 being personal best, in each piece of the pie.

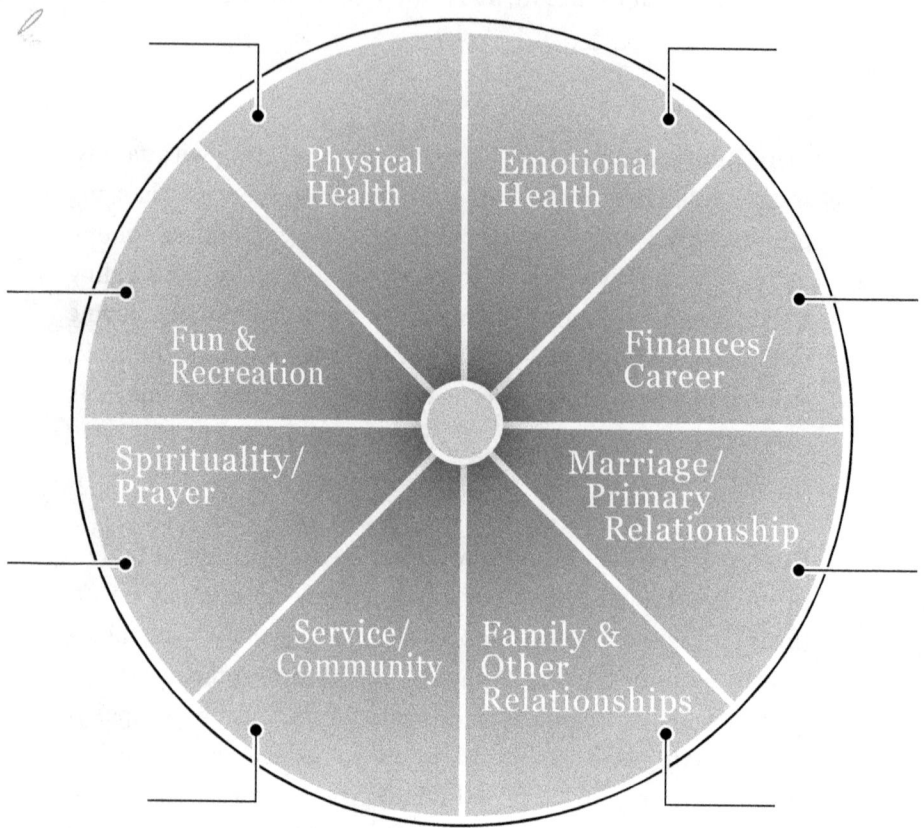

ALL RIGHTS RESERVED. THIS CHART IS THE PROPERTY OF LEADERSHIP EDUCATION ACTION PROGRAMS (LEAP) – PLEASE DO NOT DUPLICATE.

Now that you have rated yourself from 10 down to 1, it is important to notice your high scores so you can use your areas of strength to build up those areas that aren't working for you at this point. Also, notice the three lowest scoring areas. Our recommendation is to start with one low scoring area and set a goal around it with steps to improve that area (see goal-setting process in Part Two). Re-rate yourself from time to time as you move along your journey.

You are always at choice!

> We are what we repeatedly do. Excellence, therefore, is not an act but a habit."
>
> - Aristotle, Greek Philosopher

TESTIMONIES OF GRADUATES

Partner in Excellence (PIE) Leadership Course for Women

" When I was a 25-year-old professional seeking employment in Southern California, I had the incredible good fortune of attending my first personal development seminar. It was a prerequisite for a job I really wanted with Gloria Manchester, one of the authors of this book. She became my mentor. With eyes wide open, I began to grasp the principles of success, apply them to my life, and then noticed what a dramatic and positive effect it had on me, both personally and professionally. My participation in these courses gave me clarity for how I wanted to live my life and provided the tools to make the changes that mattered to me.

After becoming parents, my husband and I moved from California to Pittsburgh to raise our children closer to family. Longing to continue my personal growth, I searched locally—with no results—for seminars of the same caliber as I had taken in California. In 2007, I called upon my mentor to bring PIE to Pittsburgh, and it has been available in Pittsburgh every year since. Every one of my friends, most of my family members, and a host of coworkers and customers have completed it, including my daughter, Jade, who participated when she was only 19! The maturity I have seen in her since completing PIE is remarkable."

- **Marsha Murman**, Chloe's Adornments

" I feel so strongly about the experiential work I did for myself through this process, that I enrolled my sister, my niece and a few friends in PIE. My daughter also participated in STARR for teens. I am currently successful in my career, and happier and healthier than I have ever been in my life. And, by helping the authors of this book start a chapter for the nonprofit child abuse prevention program in Pennsylvania, I am living my vision of supporting disadvantaged, abused women and children in becoming emotionally and physically healthy, in spite of what happened to them. I am passionate about the future and I am committed to making a significant difference as a result."

- **Bobbi DiClaudio**, Color Code Interpersonal Skills Trainer - Emovere for Health and Fitness

> Referred by a trusted friend who had experienced this work in California several years ago, I took part in the first PIE course in Pittsburgh in 2007. Since then I have volunteered and served on staff for all subsequent courses. Although I always believed I was practicing the principles from the coursework, it wasn't until my last staffing experience that the light really turned on and I had my biggest "Aha!" The theme for this past course and staff was "This is the Moment" and it was all about living mindfully and in the present. The facilitators shared a story about a woman interviewed on Oprah who lost a child because she had a moment of unconsciousness. I suddenly flashed on something I hadn't thought about for a long time. Several years ago I had an unconscious moment with my son who was seven years old at the time. The result of this momentary lapse could have been disastrous. Ever since this staffing experience, I am committed to living my life differently and practicing the art of being in the moment. PIE provided me an opportunity to change someone's life ... my own!"

- **Beth Refosco**, Business Partners

> At the recommendation of Marsha Murman, a woman who I trust and admire, I participated in a women's leadership course in Pittsburgh in 2011 called PIE. I remember saying to Marsha, "I have no free time and I am honestly pretty content with where things stand in my life." I was not married or in a relationship at the time, which was fine with me. My professional life was and still is extremely exciting and successful, so before PIE I wasn't seriously looking for anything more. Yet, I was intrigued enough by the opportunity to break through another layer of personal and professional achievement. Since PIE, I have given myself the gift of dreaming beyond anything I had imagined, asking myself, "What do I really want that I don't already have in my life?"

Since PIE I have definitely changed my personal priorities. I am now married to the most incredible man and partner in life, who has grown children (and two grandchildren), whom I simply adore. My youngest stepdaughter completed STARR for teens in March 2012, and I was able to share that experience with her as a volunteer staff. I had the absolute joy of watching her bloom over that weekend and her light continues to shine! I am deeply grateful for the personal development work the facilitators have brought to Pittsburgh through PIE and STARR. I can honestly say it was a catalyst that dramatically changed my life for the best in less than a year! Today, I can't fathom my life without that experience." - **Candice Komar**, Attorney

❝ The most memorable experience for me in PIE was an exercise in which we were instructed to write a letter of regret and forgiveness to one person—father, mother or self. Since my dad had gone into the hospital the day that I started PIE, and I had struggled with our relationship for many years, I thought this was perfectly timed. I had longed to have an honest conversation with him and was afraid that I would miss my opportunity given his steady decline in health. Going through the exercise prepared me for what I knew I had to do. Shortly after the course ended, I had a beautiful and heartfelt talk with my dad. Not long after that, he died. We were both at peace." - **Sydnee Bagovich**, The Grammar Nerd

❝ I completed the last PIE for which the theme, "This is the Only Moment that Matters" was so powerful to me; it was all about getting conscious. I had already done a lot of work on myself as you will read in my story. After reading the manuscript, with all the other stories, I realized that each brought up a different emotion and in many ways touched on my own. I was able to feel their pain and then release what was still buried in my own unconscious mind. I will read this book over and over again until my heart sings with the freedom that comes with letting go of the negative emotions, replacing them with positive, empowering thoughts. I am much more aware to love myself in every moment, to be forgiving, to treat myself with respect, and to be patient with others. Life is a journey and I know, through the stories in this book, I am not alone. *Wisdom In RE* is one of the best books I have ever read. It's like a personal growth workshop to be experienced in my own time and space at home."

- **Sharon Allard**, Color Code Interpersonal Skills Trainer

PART 2

The wisdom in rethinking your life!

You are about to read stories from the coauthors along with several women who participated in our leadership courses over the last few years. Each woman, in order to write her scars-to-stars story, first had to reflect on her past and recognize the childhood conditioning and other regrets and disappointments that had been holding her back from living her highest hopes and dreams.

As you read through the stories, which do you find most compelling? What gives you reason to pause and rethink your own life?

Coauthor's Personal Journey of Regret and Disappointment

GLORIA'S STORY...

As stated in the beginning, at various points in our lives, we often re-enact our childhood conditioning or disappointments, and regrets. I certainly see that for myself. It is only through the personal development work I facilitate and practice, and the shifts I am willing to make as I journey through life, that I can embrace my past and write about it with some self-forgiveness. This is my story about the pain and shame of my own financial losses and how, for years, I unconsciously, carried the burden of my parent's losses, as well. My life has been greatly influenced by my childhood perceptions and my own risky behavior. How I handled the events in my life had everything to do with my innate personality, my family values, my filters, such as being last born, my negative and positive childhood events, and my life experiences. Even though our filters and circumstances are varied, the outcome can be similar for all of us.

I was born in Canada, an early baby-boomer, the youngest of three daughters. I was named Gloria, but my family called me Lola. My mother and father lost a son during a late pregnancy after my oldest sister was born and then had two more daughters. I was their last hope for a son, 12 years after my middle sister. In the personal development work I do, I have encountered many women, especially of my generation, who can identify with having been born the wrong sex. Boys were more valuable than girls because of the perceived notion at the time that they could earn more money to support families.

I got a lot of attention as a child because I was the youngest and had curly ringlets (that bounced like Shirley Temple's). I was an insomniac (I still am). It took the whole family, my mother, two teenage sisters, and finally, my dad, after working late each night, to rock me to sleep ... and often they fell asleep first. My dad was a hardworking entrepreneur. I adored him. I was always a naturally confident child although some might say a little "bossy," a leader in my neighborhood. I produced and directed plays (now I produce seminars). The other kids and I would put on costumes and perform for any parent who would patiently watch. Since I was pretty much an only child, I used to bring home less fortunate kids from large families for my mom to feed. When I was four years old, I took a younger child with me to the city on a public bus to see my 16-year-old sister at work in a large department store. I got into some trouble over this—an early childhood example of my risk-taking adventures. I was a Type A Personality long before we knew and understood what that was. Also, in this accounting of my life it is easy to see how many of the strengths and limitations of my Red and Yellow personality were played out early on ... and continue through adulthood.

My mom was the dominant parent in my life in that she was the disciplinarian. To punish me she would send me to my room. When she opened the door to let me out I would be standing facing the wall in the dark, refusing to come out until I was ready. As we described in the Color Code, Red is motivated by power (over events) and Yellow by fun (in relationship). That's me! Although I wasn't using Color Code in my work when my mom was alive, I am quite sure she was a Blue-Red personality (in her limitations the most controlling). Mom and I often had confrontations. Perhaps some of you will relate. I was a wild rebellious girl, and she was determined to tame me. I would go out and party and she would wait up for me and ground me for a month. On the following Friday night I would climb out my bedroom window and take off with my friends. When I returned, my good Catholic mom was still waiting up for

me and would make me swear on my dead grandmother's rosary that I hadn't had any alcohol or sex.

I gave my mother years of worry and I know she prayed for me daily. When I was 45 years old she gave me a birthday card that said something like this, *the greatest gift*

I ever gave the world was the gift of you. It was only then that I finally knew how much my mother understood my spunk, my huge heart for others, and my dream of making a difference in the world to prevent child abuse and domestic violence. I was one of the women featured in the book, *Fearless Women-Fearless Wisdom* published by Mary Ann Halpin, a renowned Hollywood photographer. I wrote in my short story about how, at the age of five, I walked in on my best friend being raped by her father. That image has stayed with me my entire life and continuously inspires and moves me to be a fearless warrior in the prevention of child abuse.

When I was 12 years old, I saw the pain of my parents almost losing their business and life savings. Everything they owned was ready to be auctioned off, when, at the last possible moment, my oldest sister's husband put enough cash together to save them from total financial ruin. As a young daughter, I felt completely helpless. I didn't realize how long I had carried the negative image of that day in my heart and mind until the incident was triggered in a seminar, years later. I never wanted to struggle like my parents did. As a natural risk-taker, I wanted to make my mark in the world by making big money. I perceived making big money was a man's game and I played it out. I would accomplish something and that little voice inside my head would be saying, "Hey Dad, am I like a son now?" The truth is, my heart was really longing for my dad's approval of me as a woman. There were years it worked for me and years it didn't. Even though I saw the pain of my parent's losses, and I consciously knew I wanted something different, unconsciously, I created the same struggle and pain a few times over again.

I raised an amazing son and daughter as a single mother, in spite of all my mistakes. Even though my children's father and I got divorced when they were young, he has always been active in their lives and we remain good friends today. In fact, my ex-husband and his wife are two of my best friends, and we are family. Since my parents were married 56 years, before my dad passed away, the breakup of my marriage was a huge disappointment to them and to me. We were both young with two small children when my husband cheated and there was a lot of emotional pain around it; however, we consciously practiced forgiveness together as a family. As a matter of fact, years after our divorce, my ex-husband generously rescued me financially, more than once. We also participated in personal-growth seminars as a family; our children started as young as 10. That has served them very well into adulthood. They are both champions in their own lives, and have given us four healthy, beautiful grandchildren, each with their own personalities. I also spent 10 years with a very successful man and two step-sons who were a little older than my children. At one point in time, we were each building a new business and raising four teenagers. It was stressful!

I have overcome so much in my life and learned from both the blessings and the adversities. My parents and sisters have all passed away and I am now the matriarch, with many nieces and nephews. My parents left our whole family a huge legacy of love and support.

It wasn't until I worked with Dr. John Gray, who wrote the best-seller *Men Are from Mars, Women Are from Venus* that I realized I was still unconsciously thinking like a Martian (thinking like a man). By nature men are the givers and women are to receive and give back; however, I was giving, giving, giving to build myself and others up. I was still seeing men as more valued than women, especially in the business world.

I was very ambitious, so in my 40's I left my professional mentor and his company to start my own financial services business. At one point, I had 15 employees and we were thriving, so I cofounded a 501 (c) (3) nonprofit organization called CARTE. It would have been enough to stop there; however, I didn't. In addition, within the same time period, I also started a personal development seminar business, aptly named LEAP. I was literally taking one *leap* after another.

Not long after, I found myself fighting for survival after my partner stole a hundred thousand dollars from our business account. I was devastated. This started a whole series of crushing events for me. I finally got rid of the partner and sold the escrow agency. The buyer paid the deposit and was supposed to make monthly payments for three years, but he never made one payment. I had paid off the business debt, but I was dependent on the income from the new buyer while I pursued my dream with CARTE and LEAP. My attorney had not secured my interest, so I walked away from a thriving business with nothing. I filed bankruptcy. I now had to totally reinvent myself professionally.

I spent a few years marketing John Gray's relationship seminars to raise funds for the prevention of child abuse. With the funding we produced accelerated self-esteem programs for abused high-risk teens through the nonprofit CARTE. In 1991, John Gray helped facilitate our first STARR Super Camp. I had a clear mission: I would produce personal-growth experiential seminars for teens and women. At this point, I engaged the professional support of Rose Gibbons, a Licensed Marriage Family Therapist with her own practice, and, like myself, a graduate and enthusiastic advocate of the personal-growth industry.

> There is a secret psychology of money. Most people don't know about it. That's why most people never become financially successful. A lack of money is not the problem; it is merely a symptom of what's going on inside of you."
>
> — T. Harv Eker: an author, businessman and motivational speaker

I seemed to grow the most emotionally and spiritually when I lost the most financially. What was going on inside of me, holding me back, were the failures of my past. As a result, coming back from financial ruin took enormous passion, determination, and energy. When the market was right, I re-entered the escrow business. However, in 2001, all the stress of my financial situation brought on the painful onset of Rheumatoid Arthritis.

Re-inspired—Re-invented ...

In 2007, I had to have a Pacemaker put in to keep my heart beating consistently. This little piece of equipment continues to save my life every day. When I am feeling most stressed, I simply take a few deep breaths, put my hand on my chest to feel the beat of my heart ... grateful that I am alive. That same year Rose and I developed the curriculum for PIE, a personal-growth and leadership course for all women. Although I had been coaching women and teens through our nonprofit work for a number of years, I wanted the professional certification, so I also started an intense training program. This was about reinventing me by choice rather than circumstance. I knew that all of this was what I really wanted to do for the rest of my life and I was going to set myself up to successfully do it.

Today, I am a nutritional and emotional intelligence life coach and seminar facilitator. I am passionate about the people I love—and all those I encounter in my practice and courses—being physically healthy (free from disease) and being emotionally healthy (free from regret). We teach what we want to learn!

I was always setting new goals around making money, winning at it most of the time. Making money always seemed easy for me, managing and keeping it certainly was another issue. I was earning over $100,000 a year in the late 1980's. That is equivalent to over $250,000 today. In 2008, I was again doing well financially, working with a few escrow accounts and building my coaching business. In the housing and financial services crash of that year, like everyone else in the industry, I went from abundance to almost no income from that source. I learned the hard lesson of what we resist persists. I had never been practical about saving for my financial future, in the past I was spending money foolishly. I was always generous and lived well, spending what I had as I made it—arrogantly thinking I could always make it again. During my peak-earning days, I once walked into a Ford dealership with my two kids and, right on the spot, bought three new cars at once, one for each of us.

In the beginning, when I was doing my own personal-growth work and hit a wall, I asked myself, "Why is it so difficult to recognize how I am sabotaging my progress, while I am doing it—what is holding me back from fully living my dreams?" I knew better. I had spent the time, money, and energy to develop myself; yet, unconsciously, I still found ways to resist changing. After all my losses, *I hurt so much I had to change.* I had to change my perception of the past, my habits, and my goals. If I was to be a success and a catalyst for change in the world, I had to change my story. This is the driving force that motivates me to produce personal-growth seminars and to coauthor this book.

My friend and organizer of our courses, Kristi, tells me I used to be known as a shit disturber and now I am known as a shift disturber. Everything I do with the courses and coaching is about boldly encouraging others to change what isn't working in their lives, and that's what *RE* is all about as well. If your job isn't working for you, make the shift and reinvent your career. If you feel depressed and hopeless, go do something for someone else in need. Regroup. To paraphrase Mother Teresa, we can't be depressed and in service at the same time. Light and darkness cannot co-exist! If your marriage or any relationship isn't working for you, reassess and recommit, change yourself or change the situation. Get out of judgment or step out!

Today, my friends and early graduates of PIE will tell you, I am now so much more tender and accepting of myself and others. As a practicing Christian woman and a Red personality I am learning more to let go and let God. I know I can't control everything in my life. I live in the moment and control what I can, in that moment. A quote of Rose's, my coauthor, is so powerful for me here, "Forgiveness is not a single act of courage, it is an ongoing act of grace." I look at myself through the eyes of forgiveness each day, give myself some grace, and thank God for my blessings and adversities.

I can now sit still for more than a few minutes at a time to pray, meditate, and do some nightly EFT (Emotional Freedom Technique). I talk

openly with my children and their spouses. I can sit with my grandchildren watching a movie, play games, and read with them ... making these some of the best moments of my life. In fact, being a grandma (the kids call me GG for Grandma Gloria) is my favorite job of all time. I can cook a healthy gourmet meal for my family and friends and feel enormously proud with the results. I have a rich life filled with love and support from family and friends.

I can also facilitate a course with women and teens and get great satisfaction watching them get the message, leaving the course excited and empowered with a better understanding of who they were born to be. One of my mantras is—what you think of me is none of my business. I don't operate on wanting to please or impress. In my limitations as a Red personality, I was doing more and feeling less. In my new story, I am continuously growing, seeking to be authentic with others, and true to myself.

Through my own discoveries, I came to realize that no matter how much I resisted, change was inevitable! I now embrace change much more quickly when some area of my life is not working. It is always a sign I need to engage in doing something differently. That is the majesty of the concept "Rethink Everything." I also know that suffering is optional! I have had many regrets and disappointments around my own personal failures. Even though I have done all this work on myself, I still occasionally do a little suffering before feeling the heat of consciousness again. I now recognize my shit sooner ... and shift.

This is what our courses are about and that's what *RE* is about. I coauthored this book to support you in achieving success as you move forward in life, no matter what you believe may be holding you back. My message is, "Don't let anything stand in the way of your dreams, especially not your own self-sabotage. Recognize it early on, and be willing to shift and move on." Let *RE* be your guide.

We, as facilitators and authors, never give students or readers anything to do that we are not willing to do first. I have completed every exercise in this book to gain fresh perspective, rethink areas of my own life, and make the changes I need to make for myself. There is no magic wand in life. SHIFT HAPPENS only in conscious choice. This book is a call to action. Exercise your power of choice and rethink your life. Take bold personal action and make the necessary changes and choices to fully live your dreams, as if you absolutely knew you could not fail.

Financial/Career Goal Exercise

Do you have a career or financial story of regret and disappointment? Are you an asset, a valuable player in your organization, job, or profession? How much value do you place on yourself? Are you ready to break through the limitations holding you back from creating new resources for increased income?

Many very successful self-improvement facilitators and authors such as Anthony Robbins, Brian Tracy, or Dave Ramsey often communicate the importance and effectiveness of having written goals. Written goals bring clarity, focus, and direction. When we take our mental goals and write them out, we not only make them more tangible, they reaffirm our intentions. It is also a powerful reminder we can use to stay on the right track when we feel stressed and more likely to make impulsive decisions. We do an exercise in the courses that demonstrates this concept, *when our intention is clear the mechanisms will appear*. When we have clarity of purpose, the steps to achieve our goal will creatively appear. Stay open to the possibilities, there are an infinite number of ways to get where you want to go.

Creating a SMART Goal

In order to succeed at anything, you must keep the goal in full view every day. The following is an example of a powerful **SMART** goal.

To – Action (To earn an additional $1,000 per month with my new enterprise)

Potential Barrier – A limitation (write something that might hold you back such as: procrastinating, having self-doubt, allowing distractions, and so on)

Steps – Create 10 specific steps to your goal (consider the mechanisms of how you will get there to accomplish what you say you want)

Daily Affirmations – End your goal sheet with an affirmation, one that will inspire you daily to stay on purpose

A **SMART Goal** stands for **Specific** (a clear and focused intention), **Measureable** (it has a start and ending), **Achievable** (it is not just a nice idea), **Risk** (it stretches you beyond your comfort zone), and it has a **Timeline** (a specific date by which you will complete it).

By applying these steps, over time and with practice, you will attain the results you want. With the support and accountability of a professional life coach and/or partnering with a trusted friend, you are significantly more likely to achieve your goal. Go to www.wisdominre.org/resources.

Steps (Examples/Ideas)

- Develop a creative marketing plan for my business idea
- Develop a presentation for women's groups to promote plan
- Create a budget of my current income and expenses (to clarify my starting point)
- Create projections for income and expenses for new revenue

- Follow up quarterly with my budget and projections (recalibrating to make sure I am on track)
- Hire a professional coach to hold me accountable and support me in achieving my goal
- Reward myself and acknowledge the small victories along the way
- Maintain a daily gratitude list of three things I appreciate about myself, as well as others who have supported me
- Post my goal with steps and my affirmation on cards or poster, placed in highly visible places around my home or office and in my purse

Affirmation (Example) – For the purpose of this financial goal, develop an affirmation that is the opposite of your potential barrier. For example, if you tend to *procrastinate*, affirm your commitment by adding *determined or action-oriented* in your declaration.

On a separate sheet, 3X5 card, or poster board write a goal, for yourself.

> It all comes down to this: if your subconscious "financial blueprint" is not set for success, nothing you learn, nothing you know, and nothing you do will make much of a difference."
>
> T. Harv Eker - an author, businessman and motivational speaker

For more details on how to set and complete smart goals go to resource page at www.wisdominre.org/resources

In a "New York Minute" Everything Can Change: Coauthor's Story of Recovery

> "Never be afraid to trust an unknown future to a known God."
> – Corrie Ten Boom

ROSE'S STORY...

In late November 2011, Gloria and I held a teleconference for the next PIE staff. In order to prepare this volunteer staff for their role in the class, we presented an exercise to create urgency in their lives and to meaningfully impact their personal relationships. We had them imagine that they were lying on their death bed and were to choose only five people in their lives to whom they wanted to impart their final expressions of love and affection. For the next staff teleconference, scheduled in January 2012, the staff's homework was to write their own eulogy, what they hoped others would say about them after they die and the legacy they wanted to leave for their families and the world. Because we, as facilitators, never have staff or students do anything we are not willing to do first, I wrote my eulogy and sent it to Gloria. I couldn't have known then, that less than a month later, I would virtually be living out this exercise.

As Christmas and the weeks leading up to it were filled with work, family, friends, and holiday activities for both Gloria and me, we decided to schedule a few days after the Christmas holiday for me to fly to her home in Northern California to focus on this book.

I would like to set the stage for what happened on December 28, 2011. At the time I was 60 years old and for years I had lived a healthy Southern California lifestyle. I exercised and took Pilates classes a couple of times a week. For some 30 years I have enviably maintained the same weight. Although there were many people in my childhood who influenced me and shaped my pursuits as an adult, two stand out, my father and my grandmother, after whom I am named. My father was intellectually brilliant, a member of Mensa and a graduate student in psychology of perception. He assessed all the children in the family on their intellectual abilities. To him I was a question mark and of average intelligence. As my grandmother's namesake I enjoyed a loving, warm relationship with her as a young child. In my teens she came to live with us when she was in the early stages of dementia. This vibrant, bright woman who used to be a fabulous teacher mentally deteriorated before my eyes. As a result, since my teens I have been captivated with neuropsychology, brain development, and emotional-social intelligence. Although I was naturally physically adept, I pushed myself intellectually to not only earn bachelors' degrees in psychology and sociology I went on to earn a master's degree in counseling psychology and licensure as a marriage family therapist.

I am passionate about the work I do in two very meaningful arenas. In our PIE and STARR courses for women and teens, I provide a safe, clinical, and powerful context for the participants to reclaim their self-esteem and rebuild their lives. And daily, as a Team Decision Making facilitator through my work in Social Services, I am instrumental in generating strength-based decisions with the families and community partners involved in the prevention and treatment of child abuse. Yet, it is my faith that sustains me. In the morning, it is the compass that I reset; and at night, it is the comforter I pull over my shoulders.

So what happened at the end of December? Just before the holidays I had gotten food poisoning and as a result I vomited numerous times. In the following days when I had no appetite, little energy, and my ribs were sore, I attributed it to having thrown up a lot. So with a commitment to get this book moving forward, I flew to Northern California as planned on December 27th. That night I had difficulty breathing. The next morning Gloria took me directly to the ER ... and in a "New York Minute" everything changed! Everything!

Within minutes a specialized team was filling me with fluids and several antibiotics as apparently I had severe Sepsis, a potentially deadly medical condition that is characterized by a whole-body inflammatory state. Days

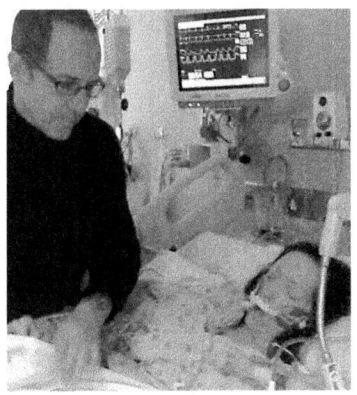
before, when I was throwing up, I had actually aspirated (breathed in) vomit into my lungs. They were now over two-thirds obstructed. I was diagnosed with Acute Respiratory Distress Syndrome (ARDS), a serious reaction to an acute infection in the lungs, which is often fatal. I also had severe pneumonia and because I could not breathe on my own, I was subsequently put on life support. All these medical terms were not only foreign to me, but I had no idea of the urgency and critical nature of the situation.

What I learned later was that once Sepsis inflames the body, for every hour that passes the mortality rate increases by 7%, if not immediately responded to with fluids and antibiotics. My life was precariously hanging in the balance.

As I was heavily sedated and being bombarded with medication, I have no memory of the first several days of hospitalization. I don't recall seeing anyone—not my son, Blaine, my brother, Stuart, or several close friends that were holding vigil at my bedside. The first time I gained memorable consciousness, I found myself lying in a hospital bed with a tracheostomy (a hole in my throat) and dependent on a ventilator to breathe. I was completely disoriented, but for my sister Heather's face. She is a former ICU nurse who lived in Alaska and had flown down to my bedside in the second week. I mouthed, "What happened?" She explained what had taken place since the day I walked into the ER. Until then, I literally had no idea it was now 2012. During Heather's one month stay, she constantly translated the medical jargon for me, interpreted my vital signs, and helped normalize my experience. As the medication and sedation were reduced, my mental clarity and acuity increased. I began to put events into some coherent and realistic perspective.

In the meantime, Gloria's house became "Command Central". She prepared healthy gourmet meals and sent email updates on my condition to family and friends. Relatives and friends, who flew in from all parts of the U.S., were fed, showered, and had a place to sleep.

Rethink Everything ...

My sister, who is a very different personality than me, (she is a Yellow) had plastered pictures and notes on the wall in front of me. In my need for symmetry and a clutter-free environment (I am a Blue Personality), the only items I wanted to keep up on the wall were a picture of my son, and a picture of me as a healthy woman waving from Air Force One (taken at the Reagan Library only two months prior).

Gloria brought in a few affirmations written on 3x5 cards to place at my bedside. One of them, RETHINK everything! was taken off a t-shirt my son was wearing the night before. Once Gloria saw it, it immediately became our mantra, not only for me, but for the upcoming PIE and STARR courses for teens. I had to rethink everything ... my whole life had changed in a matter of a few days!

My entire focus was reduced to taking a single breath in and out. Though I could initially take in a short shallow breath, I did not have the strength or ability to push the air out again. I was on a ventilator for much of the following month. Louise Hay, author of *Heal Your Body* says that the lungs represent the ability to take in life. She states an affirmation in overcoming lung problems is "I take in life in perfect balance." I was clearly out of balance and short of breath.

In the hospital I put into practice the same tools and principles I have consistently used in my personal life and in our personal development courses. And since I did not know what I did not know, I had no limitations in my mind to hold me back from full recovery or the process and timeline of what that looked like. I refused to focus on what I couldn't do or what was not working! And I expected that with a positive mental attitude, exercise, and discipline, I would reclaim my brain, body, heart, and lungs.

I had a few terrifying moments when I not only realized that I could not speak, but I struggled to transfer the thoughts in my head into legible words on paper. I knew I had significant lung involvement, as I was trached and ventilated; however, I had not yet considered the impact or possible trauma to my brain. As I could not talk or articulate my frustrations, family and friends kept telling me to just write on a white board the main words and they would get it. Though I struggled to retrieve words I knew and easily used before my hospitalization, I insisted on streaming several words together. My whole life had been dedicated to being a model of health in mind, body, and spirit and an interruption in the dynamics of abuse. I now felt like a stroke victim! What once was my Dad's question mark of my cognitive ability had now become my own. And, I had no way of expressing that struggle to anyone!

A driving force for me in my recovery was borne from the knowledge that my son had seen me on life support, in such a critical, life-threatening condition. He then had to return to duty and a rigorous training program, not knowing if I was going to live or die. As a mother, one of my greatest joys is seeing my son passionately living out his goals and dreams. Faith, prayer, conversations with God, bedside notes to family and friends, a positive attitude, Pilates exercises in bed, and walking on the unit were all strategies in my conviction and call to action. I was bound and determined to recover! I was re-establishing my independence, one measured step and breath at a time.

As I knew Blaine had gotten an emergency leave for January 18th, my intention was to make sufficient progress such that my son would see me in a healthier condition then he did at the first of the year. The hospital staff realized the importance of this goal for me and the driving force behind my efforts. Though I had made excellent progress and was looking forward to my son's arrival, just hours prior, I had a bleed-out. I was coughing up blood, as well as spurting and spewing blood through my trachea. The blood thinners used to treat the blood clot in my arm were now working against me. The medical team advised my family and friends, "It doesn't look good." In dismay, shock, and numbness, out of state relatives and family were contacted. A chaplain was called to my bedside. My sister and her husband escorted my 87 year-old mom out from Texas. Many years ago my family had already lost my oldest brother in Sacramento and now, in the same month that we lost him, they were called to my bedside. It was an eerie and uncanny remembrance.

Blaine and his dad were informed of my critical circumstances as they drove up from Southern California. Gloria told me later that I had been quite sedated and had been going in and out of sleep since the bleed-out. Around the time the nurses expected Blaine, they decreased the sedation. Gloria was with me, when my son came down the hall toward my room. I could feel his presence. When he rounded the corner into my room my eyes flew open and I mouthed my son's name. Gloria burst into tears as he approached my bed and took my hand. I still feel the effects of that heartfelt intuitive connection, and that reunion. It is the only memory of that day that I have. The rest is a blur, even the bleed-out. My son then authorized a blood transfusion. It saved my life. I was revived and re-energized!

Medical personnel had told Gloria that 95% of patients with what I had don't make it out of ICU. Heather said in 35 years of nursing she had never seen anyone survive the seriousness of my illness. The connection and irony between the exercises we had our volunteer staff do at the end of November, and what I was now facing, did not escape anyone.

However, within four weeks I was discharged from both the hospital and a short stay in a skilled care facility. By that time my trachea was removed and I was sufficiently ambulatory to take care of my basic needs. When my primary physician saw me for the first time, after having reviewed my chart, because of my obvious rapid recovery, she thought she had the wrong patient in the examination room.

I recuperated at Gloria's for a couple of months, indulging in her healthy gourmet cooking. My dear friend Victoria, a Master Pilates Instructor, flew up from Southern California to design an exercise program and coach me in reconditioning my muscles. I headed home in mid-April 2012. But prior to leaving, I returned to both hospitals to thank the nurses and doctors for saving my life. They were absolutely stunned by my level of recovery – both physically and mentally. I weighed my pre-existing weight and I had kick-started an accelerated course of recovery! Two weeks later, I marked my full return to work wearing heels and clothes I had not worn in four months. The question mark that my father had about me in my youth, and I had in the midst of attempting to accurately express my words and thoughts, was now all but erased.

Throughout my life I have been in service. As a teen I volunteered as a candy striper; I was a Volunteer in Probation (VIP) working with youth; and for some 20+ years I have donated time and expertise to CARTE and LEAP. I have formed and nurtured many significant relationships. One of the greatest blessings and biggest take-a-ways for me in my journey was the realization that I had developed a huge safety net of family, friends, and colleagues that was there for me every breath and step of the way. But for God's grace and my active faith in the healing process, I would not be here today. The biggest gift I can give in return is to continue to encourage women and teens in our work to build their own safety nets of support.

So what is the purpose of telling you my story? When we truly realize that anything can happen to us, at any time, that in a "New York Minute" everything can change, it drives home the need and urgency to get conscious, to ask ourselves, "What are my values? How do I want to live the rest of my life?" The truth is there is no certainty in tomorrow; the present is the only moment there is; and it is only in this moment that we can consciously be at choice! Through a "New York Minute" exercise in our courses the participants have the opportunity to rethink their values, their priorities, and who and what really matters to them. The process encourages participants to rebuild and revitalize relationships, to recommit to their hopes and dreams and to live life fully.

My intention in coauthoring this book is to give you a GPS, a navigational guide as you travel your own life journey. Just reading it will give you pause to reflect; doing the exercises will put you right in the middle of a process that just might re-ignite your world! Though not everyone will have a "New York Minute" like the one I experienced, many things in life are out of our control and change is inevitable! Take this opportunity now to rethink everything, to re-story your life, and to build your own safety net of love and support.

EXERCISE – BUILDING THE NET

In the space below, name five people in your life who you would include in your safety net of support. Who would be there for you? What do you need to do to further develop those relationships in order to feel fully supported and have peace of mind? What would you now want to communicate to those five people?

BOBBI'S STORY

Trusting the Process ...

In order to make positive changes in your life and realize the success you seek, you must first trust yourself and trust the process. If you have experienced childhood abuse, abandonment, alcoholism or other addiction, divorce or personal failure of any kind, your ability to trust will have been challenged, if not eroded. Unless you are willing to get honest and take a serious look at yourself ... you will never really be free to experience your full potential. Following Bobbi's story is an exercise that will assist you in recognizing how negative circumstances and events in your past may be limiting you today.

Bobbi is one of the early graduates of our PIE courses and she has continuously amazed us ... right from the beginning. She is small and mighty, a Red-Blue personality all the way. She came into the course on day 1 of 3, as she describes in her story, referred by a volunteer graduate she hardly even knew. She trusted her instincts and leaped right into the process.

Her original main goal in coming to PIE was to revitalize her career. She shares in her story that, at the time, she was also in a relationship with a man who loved her with all his heart, but she was emotionally unavailable for him and afraid she was sabotaging a good thing. As often happens, without realizing it, participants come into the course to address one issue in their lives, and some very different issues come up for them in the process. That was so with Bobbi.

The man she describes in her story has a young daughter. Bobbi didn't think she was ready for the responsibility at the time. Typically around the end of day two in PIE we count the number of children represented by the mothers in the class. We do this to bring to light the number of children whose lives will be positively affected when their moms make different choices, and begin to fully live their own potential. On the night of the count, Bobbi did not shout out her fiancée's daughter in the mix of children. When she came in the next morning, after journaling and processing through her thoughts, her heart and mind were reopened. She shared that she knew in loving and marrying this man, she would inherit a young daughter whose parents shared joint custody. We added her name in the count as one of the children that would be affected by the changes Bobbi was about to make.

Bobbi made a commitment that day in the course to re-engage with her fiancée's daughter at a totally different level. Bobbi later enrolled her husband's former wife in a PIE course—all of us knowing she was dying of cancer. She subsequently did pass away. Bobbi is now a remarkable full time mom to a teenage daughter who completed our STARR for Teens in 2012.

Bobbi continues to volunteer for our nonprofit causes and has been on staff for every PIE course since she completed her own. She also started training to be a facilitator and coach. Her vision is to be a model—a light for disadvantaged children and women. She has volunteered with CARTE on two of our most recent projects: an accelerated, experiential, self-esteem course for abused high-risk teens; and one for women victims of domestic violence.

Some of you may relate to Bobbi's story. We hope you realize that even though you have had negative circumstances in your life that may be holding you back today, you can now make different choices and change the outcome.

You must find the place inside yourself where nothing is impossible." Deepak Chopra, author and authority in the field of mind-body healing.

Today, Bobbi is a successful wife, mother, and business woman because of her willingness to look deeper inside of herself, and because she had the courage to make the necessary shifts to live a renewed life.

Bobbi's Story ...

I was born to high school sweethearts, a middle child of five, in what started out as a middle class family. Dad worked as a postman, played softball, and had his regular bowling night. My mother was a stay-at-home mom for the first few years of my life. After several years in the PTA, coaching cheerleading, and teaching catechism classes, my mom got a little restless. By the time I was in the 3rd grade she was tending bar in a local club. My parents were both drinking heavily and things started to get what I would call "crazy". Many nights they came home, and major battles ensued, which regularly ended with police involvement. At one point my father so violently struck my mother, she ended up hospitalized with a broken jaw. Until the last few years, I blocked much of those painful memories and never really considered that I came from domestic violence.

To put it in true perspective, if you were to ask any of my siblings about our family life, they may all have a slightly different understanding. At minimum, all five of us have experienced the negative effects of alcoholism, neglect, violence, and abandonment during my parent's separation and eventual divorce. At a very young age, I distinctly remember the day my father finally pulled away from home for the last time. All five of us were standing there in tears, begging him not to go. It was heart-wrenching. Those nights of fighting didn't seem to matter ... we just wanted our family together. As a child I simply didn't understand.

After my father moved out, we eventually lost our childhood home and began moving from apartment to apartment. I changed schools seven times between fourth grade and my high school graduation. We kids often came home from school to discover there was no electricity because mom couldn't pay the bill. There were times when it was so cold in the winter, that at night we would all sleep in the same bed to stay warm, in the one room of the house or apartment where we kept the kerosene heater. Having a telephone was a luxury we were rarely able to afford, and there were no cell phones in those days.

Some of my most anxious memories are those when we would be huddled in the house, as quiet as could be, while the repo man or utility companies were knocking at the door to take whatever they could or shut off our services. Definitely my worst memory was when we were living in the projects and got pad-locked out of our apartment for non-payment of rent.

Though I often felt alone and abandoned and counted on my older sisters to take care of me, by age 11, I became self-sufficient. I remember shoplifting for food to fill the emptiness in my stomach. I shoplifted for anything else I needed and wanted. It seemed to be the only way to get the things that other kids took for granted.

As a pre-teen I ate for comfort. I mixed up government issued ingredients to make things like pie dough. I would take bread, smash it in my hands then mix it with large blocks of what we called welfare cheese. In my early teens when hanging around with my sisters and their friends, I began to experiment with drugs and alcohol. I wanted to fit in somewhere, anywhere. By the age of 13, I was terribly overweight. I started crash dieting. I drank every weekend and smoked pot just about every day, before, during, and after school. When I eventually started dating, I started doing even more drugs. Drugs like acid and cocaine were not uncommon in my circle of friends and were almost always included in our weekend parties. It was all about sex, drugs, and rock and roll. Though I did what I wanted to and had few boundaries, I never had a curfew or bed time, yet I still managed to get through school with relatively good grades.

By the time I finished high school I lived with a boyfriend seven years older than me. I was pretending to be a grown woman and wife. I didn't interact with my classmates, go to the prom or even have a circle of friends my age that I could relate to. They all seemed immature to me. But in order to feel worthy I had to have a man around to love me. I now see that this was one of my limiting beliefs about myself.

As I continued to lose weight I realized men found me attractive. I reversed roles with them. I behaved abusively and attempted to control them. I gathered them and then deceived them. I saw them as objects of my conquest. The more men I attracted and conquered, the more valued I thought I was. It was crazy, so many of my beliefs were shaped by my childhood conditioning – don't trust others, hold your fears and insecurities tightly, never be vulnerable or ask for support. I was run by my fears of being rejected and abandoned, so I was determined to hurt and reject men first. In later years, after therapy and other self-improvement programs, I realized I had some healing to do with my father.

I had always counted it a blessing that I had never been sexually or physically abused. Wow, when I really got conscious and realized how my fears were dictating my life, I recognized how I was abusing myself, physically with my weight and drug issues, and sexually with my repeated conquests and rejections of men. I saw how my destructive behavior and patterns 'fed' my fears. I was now determined to turn myself around and take better care of myself.

It was a very slow process. Having struggled with my weight and body image for as long as I could remember, I started to exercise. Immediately, I loved the way it made me feel; however, I was still vying for male attention. This led to several failed relationships; so this is when I started to see a therapist. Through my therapy I gained enough confidence and self-esteem to take a job out of town and change my scene. But it didn't take long for me to go back to my old habits. I had packed my destructive beliefs along with me. I was still feeling broken, in a lot of emotional pain, and was desperately attempting to keep my life moving forward, at least professionally.

Rediscovering—Re-affirming ...

About this time, I was in a relationship with a man who loved me with all his heart and, once again, I was emotionally unavailable and sabotaging it. I almost lost him. I had never learned to build trusting and healthy relationships. Miraculously, I heard about the PIE course for women from a casual acquaintance. I participated in PIE in Pittsburgh in 2007 and got a renewed understanding of who I am and why I do what I do. I realized how a simple change in perspective can change everything. I recognized that I could thrive in this world and be in contribution to others. I stopped judging others as naïve or immature. As a result I have developed many new dynamic friendships with women. I have forgiven my parents. This choice was the most powerful gift I gave myself! It has freed me from my past. I now have a new lease on life. I feel strong, confident, and value myself as a woman. I am now married to the amazing man I mentioned earlier who still loves me unconditionally. We share a beautiful daughter, an amazing home, and the cutest little dogs. Though my past circumstances will never change, how I see them today has changed greatly.

I feel so strongly about the experiential work I did for myself in PIE, I enrolled my sister, my niece, and a few friends. My daughter also participated in STARR for teens. I am currently very successful in my work and I am living my vision—to support disadvantaged women and children in becoming emotionally and physically healthy, in spite of their past circumstances. I am passionate about the future and I know, as a result, I will make a significant difference in the world.

EXERCISE – LIMITING BELIEFS

Kevin Costner spoke at Whitney Houston's funeral about the time they worked together on *The Bodyguard*. He recalled that she needed constant re-assurance and approval asking, "Am I good enough, am I pretty enough?" As talented and beautiful as she was, and though at the time she was at the top of her game, we know now that Whitney Houston had many limiting beliefs about herself.

As with all the stories in this book, and as with Whitney, we all have negative thoughts and messages that consciously or unconsciously limit us. They hold us back from living our life to the fullest. The first step is to identify what they are.

> "Be careful how you think; your life is shaped by your thoughts."
> - Proverbs 4:23

Our brains are really an amazing creation. It would take a computer the size of the Pentagon just to carry out the basic functions of our brain. Our brains contain over 100 billion nerve cells. Each individual cell is connected with 10 thousand other neurons. Research indicates that most people speak at a rate of 150 to 200 words per minute, but the internal dialogue that we carry on with ourselves (self-talk) we do at a rate of 1300 words per minute.

You are constantly talking to yourself—all the time. In fact, you're talking to yourself right now! The problem is, in all that self-talk, you are your own worst critic. You are putting yourself down based on what others have told you or you have decided for yourself. You walk into a room full of strangers smiling, but inside you might be saying to yourself, "Am I OK? Do I measure up?" And much of this is based on our negative beliefs and experiences, what we were exposed to as children, and what we are unconsciously re-enacting today.

Get a plain sheet of paper, draw a box like the one following (as big as you need it to be) listing inside the box all the negative messages you've heard from your mother, father, others in your childhood, your husband or significant other, friends, coworkers, bosses, **or from your own negative self-talk.** All these negative beliefs are going round and round in your head whether you are consciously aware of them or not. This is what we call cul-de-sac thinking. These self-defeating thoughts are shaping your perceptions, limiting your potential, and blocking your success.

For Example
Others may have told you things such as, "You're not good enough; you're too emotional; you're not capable; you are so controlling; you are pissed-off most of the time; you are just like your mother, father, sister, brother" (comparing you negatively to someone else). Write in the box any other messages you are receiving from others that you are not OK in some way.

You may have consciously or unconsciously been telling yourself things such as, "I can't lose weight; I give up too easily; I don't have what it takes to succeed; I don't deserve it; I'm anxious all the time; I'm not pretty enough, I'm not smart enough or educated enough, I wish I was more like my brother, sister, and so on. What are you telling yourself about you?

Once you identify the limiting thoughts and beliefs (limitations) you have about yourself, as you did in the box, you will begin to recognize what is holding you back from getting what you want. This list is a first step in the process of getting conscious. As human beings, we resist change. We unconsciously allow our negative thoughts, attitudes, and limiting beliefs to dictate our lives. To the degree that you are willing to recognize and take responsibility for your choices, you can then make the necessary shifts to achieve your goals.

> Fear is the distance between the thought and the action."
> - Gloria Manchester

Each time you breakthrough your fear of change and take a different action ... **you take back your power**. The truth shall set you free! After you have reviewed your list, adding any other negative thoughts or experiences that may come up, we recommend you shred it as a symbolic gesture of letting go of those limitations. This clears the way for you to build on your strengths. As you make changes, however, you will need to recalibrate whenever necessary. The following chart was designed to support you in making the shift from the negative to the positive in any given moment.

Playing Not to Lose vs. Playing to Win - WIN/WIN

The LEAP Playing to Win Chart™ will guide you in recalibrating in your daily life. Consciously or unconsciously, most people are "Playing Not to Lose," operating from their limitations rather than their strengths. Going from the left to right on the chart you move from the **limitation** in "Playing Not to Lose" to the **strength** in "Playing to Win." For example, if you are often skeptical, consciously choose to trust more in a given situation. This does not mean you trust those that have proven themselves not to be trustworthy. In those cases, you would trust yourself to be discerning. Circle three negative attitudes on the left side of the chart where you think you show up most often. And, shift from the left to the corresponding positive attitude on the right (as needed).

LEAP PLAYING TO WIN CHART ™

PLAYING NOT TO LOSE (99% or less) operating from our limitations	**PLAYING TO WIN** (100%) operating from our strengths
Win/Lose or Lose/Win	Win/Win – 100/100
Skeptical	Trusting
Resists change	Embraces change
Reacts to world and others	Responds to world and others
Makes excuses	Accountable
Detached	Engaged
Plays it safe	Takes risks
Operates from scarcity	Operates from abundance
Wasteful	Resourceful
Meets expectations	Exceeds expectations
Gives up	Resilient
Critical	Accepting
Over-think / Over-discuss	Laser / Concise
Resentful	Appreciative
Unforgiving	Forgiving
Withholding	Transparent
Controlling	Flexible
Entitled	Grateful
Problem-focused	Solution-oriented
Self-serving	Team-player
Stuck in obligation	Stands in contribution
What is the world doing for me?	What will I contribute to the world?

www.wisdominre.org

SHARON'S STORY

Refocusing ...

Sharon's story is filled with sadness from childhood abuse. She was exposed to the physical abuse of her mother and also endured emotional and verbal abuse from most of the males in her life. Sharon was self-destructive for many years based on her limiting belief that she was not worthy. Marianne Williamson's quote seems so potent for her.

> Our deepest fear is not that we are inadequate. Our deepest fear is that we are powerful beyond measure. It is our light, not our darkness, that most frightens us. We ask ourselves, who am I to be brilliant, gorgeous, talented and fabulous? Actually, who are you not to be?"

During STARR and PIE, Sharon found the courage to look deep inside her soul, determined to take positive action to change her life. Until then she had not recognized her own power and was continually sabotaging herself.

As Sharon refocuses her energy and continues to make positive changes in her life, she displays more and more shining, brilliant moments. As she tells us in her story, "Many days I wake up to see the sunshine and feel it on my face."

Sharon's Story ...

I was born in Canada, the oldest of four children, and the only female. My parents were both alcoholics. My father was an abuser, a chauvinist, and a womanizer; and my mother was a martyr. He beat her, disrespected her, cheated on her and she just kept on taking it and having more children. One of my first memories was when I was about three or four years old, I heard my mom weeping and it woke me up. I found her in the living room on the floor with her head lying on the couch in the dark. I squeezed in, sat on her knees, and comforted her. This was the innocent beginning of my role as supporter and protector of my mom, something I continued throughout my teens. Though I was my mother's comforter, after my brothers were born, it was clear that she valued the boys over me.

A defining event in childhood occurred when I was five. I stuck a small stone in each of my ears. As my parents could not get one of the stones out themselves, they took me to the doctor. The nurses wrapped me up tightly in sheets while the doctor attempted to get the stone out. I was screaming so loudly that my dad finally entered the room to find the doctor digging in my ear with some kind of instrument. Apparently he had pushed the stone further in and I had to have surgery to have the stone removed. Though they removed it, I lost 80% of my hearing in that ear. As a result, in childhood, school, and adulthood, I never felt normal. As I heard so little, I was left out of conversations; so I was shy and confused, I felt I had nothing interesting to say. And, I never believed I was important enough to be heard.

In my youth, I lost myself in the only role that seemed to have any value to my mom and meaning for me. I was always there to protect her, save her from some beatings, and console her afterwards. But I resented her for always standing up for my brothers even though they were too afraid to come downstairs during my parent's fights.

When I was 15, in order to finish school and go to college, my aunt asked my mother to send me to California to live with her and my cousins. Once there, I began to develop normal relationships, make friends, and focus on my school work and grades. Then, just before my high school graduation ceremony, I got a phone call that changed the course of my life. My father and mother had gotten into another physical fight. This time however, my mother had stabbed my father and she had been arrested. My aunt arranged for me to return home temporarily to support my mom. Because of the record of calls the police had of my father's long history of physical abuse towards my mother, they saw the stabbing as self-defense and dropped the charges against her. She was subsequently released. Much to my aunt's dismay, I stayed in Canada near my mother, acquired my high school diploma from California, and started a pattern of destructive behaviors.

As an early teen, all my brothers' friends wanted to have sex with me and I knew it. But I didn't have my first sexual experience until I was 17, when I returned from California. After that first sexual experience I pretty much allowed men to use me. I was always disrespected by my father; he called me names and made me work extra hard for anything I wanted. I cannot remember him praising me or sitting down to talk with me. I also don't remember my mom comforting me, stopping my dad's verbal abuse, or standing up for me. For me, it seemed the only time I mattered was when I was in a relationship with a man. At the age of 18 I got pregnant. My mother attempted to get money to care for the baby, but my boyfriend would only pay for an abortion, a very painful memory for me. No one asked what I wanted, if I was OK or needed something. I was confused, scared, and in pain. Once again, I seemed to have no voice.

A few years later, I married a man and had five children (all girls). He was in love with someone else when we met and got married. I gave my whole self to him and kept giving. I never asked for my needs to be met and he totally ignored me. Intuitively, I thought something was not right, there had to be something more for me. I went to counseling for two years before I found the courage to leave my husband and raise my five girls on my own. Though I went on welfare, I applied for an entrepreneurship grant for single mothers. I had always been an extra-hard worker and I was determined to get off welfare. After a lengthy qualifying process, I was one of three women who were awarded the grant. I was honored by United Way. I now had the finances to start my own business! The grant validated me and gave me hope for a different future. My girls and I had our photo on posters and my success story was printed in newspapers and magazines.

Still, after my marriage ended, I kept on choosing men who devalued me, used me, and would not commit to me. I took myself and my daughters on an emotional rollercoaster with my choices in men and my desperate need to hold on to them. I gave myself to them whenever they wanted sex and I drank or got high to stop the pain. I also became a workaholic. My aunt said I was a codependent, like my mother. Whenever I called my California aunt, or went to stay with her at different intervals with my kids, she gave me a lot of support. She encouraged me, kicked me in the butt, and loved me unconditionally. She was my mentor and my strength so many times in my life.

At the age of 53 and freshly out of a relationship with a married man with whom I worked, my aunt called me one day and said she wanted me in the next STARR in Boise, Idaho. Though I had been to a couple of seminars before that she had recommended, she told me this one was specifically for victims of domestic violence. I know this sounds strange, but I didn't understand why I would be in this one. I wasn't in a domestic violence situation, was I? It is amazing what denial will do to someone's mind. I now realize I had been exposed to domestic violence as a child and later replayed this dynamic as an adult, allowing myself to be used and abused over and over again. One thing I remember that the facilitators said in STARR, "First time victim, second time volunteer." I now see how I volunteered for the abuse as an adult. During the course they asked me to put my hand on my heart and feel the beat of my heart; I couldn't hear or feel my own heartbeat for the longest time.

After STARR I did get some counseling for drug and alcohol abuse. I know the strength it took for me to get through the adversities in my life. I acknowledge my determination and resilience. I have worked hard to break the cycle of abuse in my own family. I am giving voice to my thoughts and feelings. I am continuing to fight for my freedom to be authentically

me. I am honoring and nurturing myself. I am refueling and giving back to the world. I got a hearing aid. I am preparing myself for a new career, sold my house, paid off my debts, and started eating more nutritionally. I am rebuilding my family relationships. My daughters are accomplished and in healthy relationships. I know they want me sober, making healthier choices, and moving forward in my life. I am encouraged by the fact that my girls got the best there is in me.

Resolving ...

To reinforce the lessons learned in STARR, I participated in the PIE leadership course for women and completed my certification as a Hartman Color Code Personal Skills Trainer. I know I am capable and valued. Even though I still have my down times, many days I wake up to see the sunshine and feel it on my face. I am learning to accept and love myself as I am, embrace my innate personality, and strive for the life I really want and deserve. Maybe telling you my story is my new beginning.

EXERCISE - A MATTER OF PERCEPTION

Sharon spent several years victimized by her feelings of inadequacy and her limiting beliefs. You may identify with her story. As we stated in the CEO Chart, our perceptions are shaped by the beliefs and core values we downloaded as children. As Wayne Dyer, author, has said, "If you change the way you look at things, the things you look at change." It is not what happens that matters most, it is how we view what happens and what we are willing to do about it. In PIE and STARR, we tell women and teens who are in relationships or situations that are not working for them, you have two options—change yourself or change the situation. You stay and shift ... or you leave. You get out of judgment or you step out! Sharon had so many things to resolve in her life, and she is doing it. Piece by piece.

Use the space below to describe a story of betrayal around a particular situation in which someone hurt you as an adult. Really play out this story as a victim, elaborating on and dramatizing the circumstances. Use this time to tell it with all the pain you felt and the powerlessness you experienced from the betrayal. This should be a story of betrayal from one adult to another. This story should take no more than three minutes to write.

Example - You were betrayed or hurt by a friend, ex-boyfriend, significant other, coworker, business partner, etc.

Now use the same story, writing it from a different perspective—taking responsible action for your part in it. We are not suggesting that you take over-responsibility or responsibility for the other person's behavior or actions. We are asking you to explore what you could have done differently in that same situation. This should take less than two minutes. Example: You heard through someone else that a girlfriend said something very negative about you that was untrue. Instead of first checking it out to see if she actually said it and resolving the conflict with an open and honest conversation, you stayed in your anger and resentment, and the relationship subsequently ended.

Using the same story, again tell it as if you are a newscaster writing an article about it, though it is nowhere near the front page. No drama, no blame, or shame. This version is not about your emotions or feelings about it. It is simply the facts. It is just what happened. This part should take less than a minute.

The purpose in writing the same story three different ways: as a victim —expanding on the blame and everything you perceive was done to you; then as a responsible participant—what you could have done responsibly different in the same situation; and finally, as a newscaster —it's simply the news, is to provide you with an opportunity to rethink your perceptions of yourself, others, or a particular situation. It is an opportunity to make a shift! Ask yourself, "Is this getting me what I want?" If it's not, do what Sharon did, resolve to see it differently.

Which version of the story was easier to tell?

Which version did you have the most difficulty with?

What were the "Aha's!" you got from this exercise?

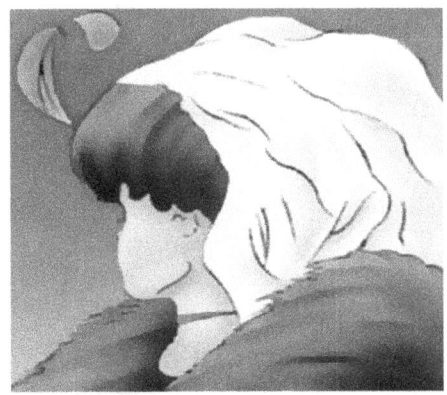

Take a look at this image. Do you see the old lady, the young lady, or both?

Old Lady _____
Young Lady _____
Both _____

This optical illusion is about perception. It doesn't necessarily matter what you see (old, young, or both) because there is a much more powerful message here. What matters is how you interpret or process and define what you see. For instance, a mother might view the picture of the young lady as representing her lovely daughter venturing out into the world; another may see the profile of a young woman contemplating her dreams; or a teenage girl all dressed up to go dancing, looking out into the night. Someone else may see the old lady first and think of an elderly woman from a cold European country wearing a scarf and fur coat; others might see a woman who has lived long and sacrificed much; or others see an old woman with head bowed in thought or prayer. There are an infinite number of possibilities and taglines, both positive and negative.

It is not the experiences and events in our lives that shape us but the lens through which our brains process the experiences and events. Positive psychology states that what actually occurs in our lives (the events) are only predictive of about 10% of our levels of success and happiness, 90% is based on the way our brains process the events. In other words, the perceptions we have about the young lady or the old lady (representing the events/experiences in our lives) and the decisions we make from them, actually determine our level of success and happiness.

Though we cannot undo our past, we can reset our interpretation of our past; we can consciously reassess our beliefs and change our attitudes. We can turn the tide of our negative thoughts and rewire our brains through our conscious efforts to reinterpret our perceptions and make healthier choices about ourselves and others.

SYDNEE'S STORY

Re-engaging—Rebuilding Relationship ...

Sydnee is the newest member of our graduating team who wrote her story for *RE*. We often hear the phrase "Timing is everything!" Sydnee was at a point in her life where she was extremely excited to participate in PIE based on what she wanted to accomplish and what she had heard from other graduates. Though she had wanted to be there eight months earlier, the fact that her Dad went into the hospital the day she actually started PIE seemed so poignant. She later discovered that PIE is where she needed to be to build her safety net of support in light of her father's illness.

Sydnee is a Blue personality driven by intimacy. Because of her commitment and courage to face the truth about the struggle in the relationship with her father, she stayed in the course for two and a half days. With other losses in her life and the potential loss of her Dad, it could have been overwhelming. Her willingness to write her letter of regret and forgiveness to her father, and to later have that honest conversation with him, teaches us all that we don't have to continue to live with regrets.

> As women we all dream of having a strong dad that loves us unconditionally. Ann Geddes' quote touches every woman – "Any man can be a father, but it takes someone special to be a dad."

Sydnee's Story ...

I was born first, three sisters followed, and then after eight years, a brother.  My dad was a blue-collar guy. Big, strong. A man's man. What I remember about him is that we didn't see him much—he worked two jobs. He was an elevator constructor during the day and had a part-time job in the evenings and weekends. When we did see him, my memories don't include much family socializing. They were more of eating with us, doing yard work, and watching sports on TV.

A fond memory is of my dad lying on the living room floor, telling us that we could have all of the change in his pockets if we would rub his back. I also remember that my parents seemed to fight a lot. I remember being in the middle of one of those arguments once, when one of them lobbed a roll of masking tape at the other, and it hit me. Then I remember, one day when they were in their bedroom with the door closed, having a serious discussion, um, fight. Just picture five kids just outside that door listening in. When my mom and dad came out, we all told them that we were sorry. "We'll be good, please don't fight." We thought that what they were arguing about was our fault.

They divorced when I was eleven.

I remember going through a rough time after that, which included chronic headaches. My mom scheduled an appointment for me at Children's Hospital. I remember seeing a neurologist, and he took me through a series of tests. "Touch your nose, then touch this pen." I met with a psychologist and talked about everything and nothing. It was determined that there were no medical issues, though I do recall feeling better after talking with someone.

Some years later I began therapy for myself. My therapist suggested that I read the book, *The Dance of Anger*. That is what prompted me to have the conversation with my dad. I told him that I wanted to meet—I had something to talk about with him. Now remember that my dad was not a sensitive, touchy-feely kinda guy. I can only imagine what he was thinking! Surely nothing that met what I had in mind! I wanted him to know that I wanted us to be closer. I wanted the father-daughter relationship of story books and movies. I wanted my dad to be involved in my life—to know what I was doing, to ask me how I was doing. I am not sure how all of those thoughts came out, and I don't remember what he said, but what I do recall was something along the lines of how I could have done more, in a sense making it my fault. And that is all that I remember of the meeting. That's all that I carried with me for a very long time after that. I loved my dad, but I knew that I would never really be close to him; well, never as I wanted us to be. What I realized many years later is that the relationship that I had with my dad was the most that he was capable of giving.

Eventually, he remarried. It was rough at first, but we adjusted. Then they had a son. That sparked all kinds of feelings. That was tough for all of us, and we slowly moved away from what little connection we had. My dad and his wife separated, and that is when he became more involved in our lives. He began coming around for all holidays and for our birthdays; he always got us together to go out to lunch or dinner. My mom and dad became civil again, and it was nice. Even though the conversations were awkward—we never had anything real to talk about with Dad, not a whole lot of common ground—still we enjoyed the family time together. Holidays became more precious.

Flash forward to December 1, 1999, my little brother Justin's 26th birthday that he would never see. My mom got the call, and then called each of us over to her home. We were all beyond shocked—screaming and crying. No! This could not be happening. Justin was our only brother. He was just beautiful and so special to us! I think that that is my first memory of my dad being emotional. He choked back tears. This big, strong man, unable to cry. I can't imagine how difficult that was for him.

Five or so years later, my sister Stephanie was diagnosed with Stage IV Melanoma, and we watched her slowly go through the phases of an ugly disease. In the end, we were all there with her, at her hospice bed in my mom's bedroom. Dad was there with us, but he stayed in the other room. He could not bear to be at the bedside as she was dying. My sisters, my mom, and I watched Steph take her last breath and were relieved to see her struggle come to an end, for her to be at peace at last. Ah, finally Stephanie could be with Justin!

So, another change to our family makeup. Another change to the family holiday and birthday gatherings. As one dies, so another is born. My youngest sister, Shawna, had a daughter at the time of Steph's death, with another on the way. After that a son, and then another son. Those kids loved Pappy! They were our new family gatherings—the holidays, the new birthdays.

In the summer of 2011, I had my first introduction to this thing called PIE. I had become friends with several women who spoke so highly of it, and I just couldn't wait the eight months before I could experience it myself! March 2012 finally came. I didn't know what to expect, but I knew that there would be transformation. Breakdowns and breakthroughs. I figured plenty of chick stuff, and I was all about chick stuff. Self-disclosure, self-improvement. Yep. That was all me! Well, on the morning of the first day of the workshop, I learned that my dad had been admitted into the hospital. He had walked in the night before with unbearable pain in his hip and leg. Just before the program was to start, I visited my dad. He was in good spirits. "So Dad ... !" We spent some time together, and then I went off to my long-awaited start of PIE.

For the next two days, I experienced the excitement of PIE—the emotional rollercoaster of all that was going on there and with my dad. During the days, I went through exercises of getting to know 24 very different women and all of their stories, learning, breaking down, hugging, crying, laughing. On breaks or in the evenings, I checked in and kept up with my dad. The most memorable exercise of PIE for me was writing a letter of regret and forgiveness to one person—father, mother or self. I thought it was perfectly timed so I chose Dad. I had to list all of the regret that I had about our relationship and then forgive—all as if speaking directly to him. I had longed for that opportunity! And, with my dad now in the hospital, I was so afraid that he would die before I could tell him how I really felt. I sobbed the entire time I wrote. Big, fat tears mottled my paper. Through heavy tears and gasping, I eventually read my letter aloud to one of my PIE sisters. Big hugs. Release. Oh, that was good! Then I shredded my paper. Finality on many fronts. This exercise was complete.

Several days after the euphoria had passed and PIE ended, I learned that Dad had cancer in the liver, and they started radiation therapy. On the final day of the radiation, further tests indicated that the cancer was actually in his lungs and in his bones. That was a different diagnosis with a completely different prognosis. Dad opted to stop treatment and move into home hospice care. Two weeks after he walked into the hospital with hip pain, he needed assistance to make it to the gurney, to be sent home via ambulance. That was indeed a sad sight. Imagine walking into a hospital with leg pain and two weeks later being sent home to die.

For about a week, Dad's ever-present quick wit remained intact. I knew that I had to have that hard conversation. I called on my PIE sisters for support. I needed them to form a virtual circle of strength and support around me. I sent them an email, and WOW... the incredible responses that I got. It was as if they were all right there with me. Each time I looked at my phone, there was another response ... and another. Rapid fire. The emotional intensity of their messages was absolutely indescribable. I heard them, I felt them as I rehearsed at least a dozen times what I wanted to say. I knew that I could do this. I had to! And, when I did, of course, it was NOTHING like the way that I had planned, but it happened. And my dad showed caring and affection that I cannot recall at any other time in my life. That said it all. That made it all worthwhile—for both of us. I knew after that moment that Dad and I were both at peace. He would rest in peace, and I would live knowing that I had been blessed to be able to make peace with my dad before he left this Earth. Two weeks after being released into home hospice care, my dad passed away softly with me by his side. I love you, Dad.

EXERCISE – A LETTER TO MY FATHER

Through the letter exercise in PIE, Sydnee used this opportunity to express forgiveness and release her regrets with her dad while he was in the hospital. It opened the door for her to have that loving, peaceful conversation with him before he passed away. That was a gift she willingly gave her dad and received for herself!

As a child we learned how to be in a primary relationship by watching our mother and father (or father-figure) in their relationship. The ways in which your father (or other male) regarded your mother is etched in your unconscious mind. As women we often recreate that same dynamic in our own relationships … whether positive or negative. To paraphrase Dr. John Gray, a woman's sense of self is often defined through her feelings and the quality of her relationships.

Some of you may have been abandoned by your father through death, divorce, and alcoholism or drug addiction. There is an absence, whether physical or emotional. If he was there, was he respectful or disrespectful towards your mother, you, or others in the household? What was the message you got from your father about you as a female? Do some journaling below to answer these questions and to raise your awareness as to your relationship with your father. Unconsciously, our relationship with our father often defines our relationship with men.

What I learned about men from my father was …

If you have any regrets and disappointments towards your father (whether he is alive or not) we recommend you write, on a separate sheet, a "Recognition Letter" to him. You will find instructions at the end of Part Two, in "The Heart in Forgiveness."

Once you have expressed and processed the anger, hurt, and regrets in the relationship you can shred it and then write a "Response Letter" to say all the things you actually wanted or longed to hear from him. Take ownership of your healing process with the understanding that your father may never change. That one shift in your perception could change everything for you in your primary relationship or in seeking the relationship you say you want.

NANCY'S STORY

Revealing the Truth ...

> As you read through Nancy's story it may be easy for some of you to identify with her emotional struggles, though your circumstances may be quite varied. She had done a tremendous amount of work for herself prior to her participation in PIE, much of it an internalized process of self-expression. In an experiential group dynamic, PIE was a catalyst for her to dig deeper to get to the roots of some of her pain and be receptive to feedback from the facilitators and other women in the course.
>
> There were a few natural events in Nancy's adult life that unearthed either painful childhood memories or sorrow-filled losses. As she revealed the truth to herself and others whom she trusted, she could then reflect on the choices she had made and embrace her remarkable determination to live her life differently—with joy, compassion, and resolve.
>
> Nancy played a powerful role as a member of the staff for our STARR course for women victims of domestic violence. She is an innate White personality—grounded and often the voice of reason. She has incredible listening skills and easily empathized with the women participants as they moved through the processes for healing and reclaiming their lives.

Nancy's Story ...

As children, my older sister and I lived in a small house with my parents surrounded by weeping willows, cherry trees, and gardens. I have a vivid memory of all the colors, the blossoms, and flowers. I also remember the day my alcoholic father started molesting me. I was only nine years old. Though I told my mother after the first incident, and kept saying, "No!" to my father, he didn't stop; and she did not protect me from him. I lived with the abuse, keeping it a secret even from friends. When I was a teenager, my mother was diagnosed as Bi-Polar, a mental illness also known as manic depressive disorder. My mother went through periods of deep depression and at other times she would be emotionally and verbally abusive. There were many memorable moments and events in my childhood that were filled with laughter and joy, but they were usually overshadowed by the fears, the sadness, and the pain I felt as a child.

Though I was destined to become a wife, mother, business manager, and "Plant Whisperer," I spent my teens and early twenties re-enacting the abusive and dysfunctional relationships of my childhood. It would be quite a while before I became known for my expertise in planting, nurturing, and caring for all kinds of plant-life. I first had to dig deep internally to get to the root of my own issues.

After a failed marriage that ended in divorce, I soon found myself lying in my bed shaking uncontrollably from what I later realized was alcohol poisoning. It was then that I finally said, "No, I've had enough of the abuse I am causing myself and others!" I wanted a monogamous relationship with someone I could trust to love me. It was around this time that I met my future husband, Michael.

Michael and friends introduced me to healthy outdoor activities—mountain biking, hiking in mountain meadows, walking among the desert flowers, and camping. Our relationship blossomed. He became my best friend. He loved me with full knowledge of my past and we were married. Once we had children we introduced them to our love of nature and continued these outdoor activities throughout their growing years.

Then the unexpected happened. When my father was married for the third time, he had a baby girl. Seeing in this birth my own childhood potentially repeating itself, I had many sleepless nights as once repressed feelings bubbled up inside of me. I read books like *The Courage to Heal* and took classes about the destructive effects of alcohol. For the sake of my new stepsister, I knew I had to confront my father and I did! I remember sitting in my father's small living room with his wife, while his young daughter played around us. Without hesitation I demanded that he get counseling for sexual perpetrators. I told him that I had never forgotten my own childhood abuse and I was not going to let this happen again. Though he had never been forced to come to terms publically or privately before, he did not deny the abuse. To his credit, he subsequently spent years in recovery.

What we reveal, we can heal."
- Rick Warren

I was 30 at this time and spent the next 10 years in counseling and group support. I felt so much pain I would run and scream in fields and cry just sitting in the bath tub. Though as a little girl my innocence had been shattered, I was now beginning to purge the resentment, sorrow, and pain. I kept a journal, I practiced meditation, and I focused on my spiritual development. I listened to my dreams, wrote letters, and poetry. I learned to set and maintain boundaries and to release negative emotions. I reparented myself, restoring the values of trust, integrity, and stability.

Even with all my new tools, when my husband went back to school full time, I was still emotionally up and down. I was struggling to cope and maintain a healthy balance while caring for our two young children. In the middle of all of this, my mother passed away. I suddenly realized I would never have the emotionally healthy mother, who should have protected me, and for whom I had longed for since I was nine. I slipped into a depression. Ironically, I was soon diagnosed with Bi-polar Type I mental illness, just like my mother. This experience was a defining moment. I finally realized I have a neuro-chemical imbalance that is not something of which to be ashamed. My mother denied her illness. To her it was a social disgrace. She was ashamed and she did not have access to today's treatments and new medications. Because I had experienced the painful impact of my mother's denial on our family, I was determined to live my life differently in the face of this disease. For the sake of me, my husband, and my children, I became fully committed to my mental, physical, and emotional health.

I responsibly take my medication. I do not drink alcohol as it harmfully interacts with the medications. I regularly meet with my psychiatrist for my health and for that of my family. And to gain the upmost benefits from the consultation and medications, my husband often goes with me to my psychiatric appointments to openly offer his perspective.

In my work, I manage a business and get to care for both indoor and outdoor plants. Yes, my clients call me "The Plant Whisperer." One such client lovingly introduced me to PIE. Although I had done a lot of personal-growth work and for years had consistently taken my medication, my interest was piqued. To my surprise during a forgiveness exercise it was not my father I saw in front of me, it was my mother. I doubled over unable to breathe. I realized in that moment, I had not done the underlying emotional work and I hated being mentally ill like my mother. During this exercise I consciously forgave her, myself, and let go of the pain and sorrow I had felt for so many years. My mother had resisted her disease, demonstrating how not to live with mental illness. I made a major shift from this painful legacy. My disease was not going to determine who I am.

Today, I see myself as a successful woman, a wife, mother, and business manager. Michael and I still walk hand in hand after over 20 years, and while raising our son and daughter. We love seeing them grow with confidence to face their challenges and the self-esteem to reach their goals. I asked our children what they liked about us as a couple and as parents. They confirmed what we strive for when our daughter said, "You both share equal power. You are committed to resolving and discussing your differences until you work them out." My son explained, "I feel there is total acceptance from you and Michael."

Restrengthening ...

I am grateful for my own courage to heal, the encouragement I have received from others on my journey, and the opportunity to be a model of a loving, healthy, free spirit. My husband and children know I am writing this story and they totally support me in the hope that it will benefit many others. I have come to realize that forgiveness is the key to happiness. This poem, written by our daughter, reaffirms the healing that I did, with Michael's supportive love, and the parenting we have done together.

I Am from Happiness

I am from a big rocking chair, from LA-Z-Boys and green fabric rocking me to sleep, as an infant in my brother's steady arms;

I am from the cold kitchen counter talking; laughing, enjoying life from my high perch above the false tile;

I am from plants galore surrounding me; they were my forest, my own little world where anything was possible;

I am from card-playing and camping with wildlife;

I am from the foothills, walking till our feet were sore with pleasure;

I am from sparkling blue eyes with a sprinkle of ginger from Nancy and Michael.

EXERCISE – MY MOTHER-MYSELF

There is an inherent link between mothers and daughters (womb to womb), a relationship that does more to define us than any other. For years Nancy had longed for a healthy relationship with her mother. As Nancy shares in her story, "To my surprise during a forgiveness exercise it was not my father I saw in front of me, it was my mother and I doubled over unable to breathe. I realized in that moment, I had not done the underlying emotional work and I hated being mentally ill like my mother."

You are much less likely to forgive yourself if you haven't forgiven your mother.

Nancy went on to say in her story, "During this exercise I consciously forgave her, myself, and let go of the pain and sorrow I had felt for so many years." Through therapy, meditation, and PIE she healed and embraced herself. Nancy handles her disease in a totally different way than her mother. As a result, she passes on a healthy legacy to her own daughter.

Consciously or unconsciously, many of us re-enact, in our own lives, our mother's unresolved issues. What we resist persists. We always ask the women in our courses, "When are you most like your mother?" Your answer could surprise you!

I am most like my mother when …

If you are harboring any resentment towards your mother, we recommend you go to the end of Part Two, "The Heart in Forgiveness" and write a "Recognition Letter" and "Response Letter" to your mother as Nancy did.

ANNETTE'S STORY

Redefining Herself ...

Annette describes in her story that as the oldest child she had to help raise her five siblings due to her mother's depression. Then she married a man who was very controlling, which left her no space to care for herself. She had been living in an unfulfilling marriage in which she believed she didn't have a voice. After her children were grown, she longed to be free of the restraints and dysfunction of her 38-year marriage.

Annette was referred to PIE by a good friend. Prior to the course, she had made the decision—PIE would be the catalyst for her to leave her marriage and move across country to be near her daughter and grandsons. Not long after the end of PIE, she told her husband she was leaving. Annette is a Blue personality who naturally desires to be in an intimate relationship. As a woman of integrity and commitment she did not take the end of her marriage lightly.

What happened next could not have been predicted. In the middle of Annette's plan to restart her life, to finally take care of her own needs, a tragedy occurred and she was sidetracked. As always, she took care of everything and handled it all with patience, dignity, and grace.

Although for a short time derailed, she continued on her journey. As a result of the work she had done in PIE, she now had the tools to rewrite her story, redefining her commitment to herself.

Annette's Story ...

I began my life as the first child of a good Catholic family that eventually grew to six children. My parents were hard working middle-class people; my Dad built our house where we grew up brick by brick. We lived in the basement while he continued to build the rest of the house as they could afford it. As my parents worked side by side, I was often left in the child swing to occupy myself. Then five more children were born. I believe this all led to feelings of abandonment throughout my life; I always held a limiting thought that I was never good enough or worthy enough.

Mom and Dad had conflicts from the day they were married. His parents never accepted my Mom due to differences in nationality and religion. My grandparents on my Mom's side died when I was three, and my Dad's parents played favorites with all the grandchildren. Since my Mom was not accepted by them, we were also not accepted. As the eldest, I always had a greater responsibility to care for the younger children. When my parents would fight, my Mom would give Dad the silent treatment and I would be the go-between. Mom suffered from depression and her antidote was sleeping; she would stay up late at night (her form of birth control after six children) and then sleep late in the morning. Dad and I were responsible for getting the younger children and me off to school in the morning, with breakfast and lunches packed. Mom would usually nap around dinner time, leaving me responsible for getting dinner on the table when Dad came home. Many nights she would sleep through dinner.

I was extremely quiet and shy at school. I was not a particularly gifted student. I struggled, especially in math. But as the first child, I was expected to go to college. The extreme stress of getting good grades caused me many health issues. I didn't date until college. Then I went on a double-date with a friend because she was afraid to be alone with her boyfriend, so she fixed me up with his cousin. I had my first sexual relationship with him and then he dropped me.

I was 19 when I met my future husband and we fell head over heels in love. On paper, we had everything going for us—same religion, same ethnic and working class background, oldest child, same career paths as teachers, and we both came from dysfunctional families. Unfortunately, we also struggled with the same self-esteem issues. I believe that when we fell in love, we thought we would fill the void with each other for the love and attention we never received as children. In view of all the past family issues and no positive relationship role models, I now see how naïve it was for us to believe that. We truly thought that together we could create a better world for ourselves, our students, and our children.

My husband was raised in a family of alcoholics and although he himself had no problems with alcohol or drugs, his drug was "control." As a good Christian wife and obedient care-taker, I allowed myself to be the object of his control. During my entire marriage, though I worked from day one, first as a teacher, then in sales, I had no input on our finances. As my two children grew, I did my best to protect them from his control, but I realized I was becoming more controlling in their defense. When they left for college, his control was solely directed at me, and we continued the power struggle. While in many ways I may have seemed complacent, I was also building my resentments and almost becoming the person I was fighting against. At this point, I had never even written a check and was still on an allowance. After 38 years of marriage, several marriage counselors, and marriage retreats, he was still convinced (and convinced me) that I was the one with the problem—I did not see the world his way. He wanted me to be totally submissive.

I suffered from a debilitating autoimmune disease, yet continued to work and hand off my paycheck to him. Yes, we appeared to have it all—big house in the country where we entertained family, friends, and church groups. We were active in our church and community. We took lovely vacations and trips to Colorado to visit the grandsons. We had successful careers and owned several rental properties. From the outside, life looked great. But my mental, physical, and emotional health were deteriorating. I had to make a change. While in therapy, I asked him to leave, but at the end of six weeks, he was even more convinced that I was the one with the problem.

At the recommendation of a good friend, I attended the PIE course for women in Pittsburgh five months before my 60th birthday. In my mind, in preparation for participation in this intensive course, I set that date as the beginning of my new life. I remember the facilitators telling us the first day, there are only three basic reasons people change—they hurt so much, they have to change; they learn so much, they want to change; or they receive so much, they initiate change. I hurt so much I had to change!

I went home and soon afterwards told my husband I was leaving. I sold off or gave away much of the accumulated household items from those many years of marriage, packed what would fit into my car, and headed off to Colorado, to live with my daughter and grandkids. On my drive to Colorado while I was figuring out the next step for myself and my career, I decided to stop in Texas to visit my youngest sister. I was excited about getting some sister support. I spent nine wonderful days with her and her husband. We talked about our lives, our marriages, our work, our insecurities, and our hopes for the future. She knew what I had been through, and in a lot of ways, she was going through some of the same struggles and challenges.

On the day before I was to leave, I went out with my brother-in-law for some last minute sightseeing. My sister stayed behind, as she said she had a hair appointment. When we returned about three hours later, we opened the garage door, and as soon as we heard the car engine and saw the vapors, we knew she was dead in the car. My life had just made a 180 degree turn and the "self" that I was just beginning to take care of had to go immediately into caretaker mode once again. I handled all the arrangements for her body to be returned to Pennsylvania, the co-signing of her husband to a mental facility for a 24 hour suicide watch, the boarding of the diabetic dog, and the notification to the family and her employer. I had to return to the home and husband I had just left to receive family and friends for the funeral and the wake. I continued as the main care-taker and organizer for the next thirty days.

Restarting ...

Once again, after it was over I headed for Colorado to find the peace and freedom I had never known, and to restart my life. I am now supporting myself financially, my health has improved, and every day I have a view of the beautiful Colorado Mountains. I also get to see and be with my grandsons. My husband and I have a better relationship now as co-grandparents, he from a distance. I have come to understand that

my sister and I both had choices in how we would handle life's painful issues. Our choices were completely different. I wished my sister would have gone to PIE with me, she might have realized she had the power to change her life rather than hopelessly end her life. Although I am often sad when I think about this, I know it was beyond my power to change the situation. I see my own future now with so much more clarity and possibility and I am very thankful for that.

> A mind that is stretched by a new experience can never go back to its old dimensions."
>
> - Oliver Wendell Holmes Jr., American writer

EXERCISE – THE NEED FOR URGENCY

In life we often miss opportunities to communicate with each other at an authentic level (coming from a deeper source of love or pain). Annette communicated to us that she initially experienced sadness and regrets after they found her sister. It is human nature to think, "What could I have said or done differently?" In suicide, ultimately the choice is theirs. However, the difference in how the two sisters handled their own life regrets is stunning! Annette's courage and her sister's story teach us so much about the need to express, in any given moment, the full extent of our love for one another, never knowing when it may be our last.

This next exercise is for you to get conscious about who in your life may not know how much you love and appreciate them. If you were in a life-threatening situation, wouldn't you express your true thoughts and feelings to the important people in your life?

Part 1 – Scenario
Imagine yourself on an airplane with 150 other people. Everything seems to be going well until you hear an unusually loud pop or bang. Then you hear the pilot on the intercom directing the flight attendants to prepare the cabin for an emergency landing in the water below. The passengers are instructed to secure their seatbelts and brace themselves for landing. You have approximately three minutes to focus on your last thoughts, prayers, or pictures in your mind. The plane could make a safe landing and you could survive, but what if you don't? You are sitting amongst strangers, not your family and loved ones.

Visualize in your mind, the most important people in your life to whom you want to silently impart your final expressions of love and affection. Who would you choose and what words of wisdom and love would you impart, if they were sitting right in front of you during this dramatic life-threatening event? Remember you only have three minutes. The plane is going down!

Part 2 – Expressions – You don't have to wait for such a scenario to occur. Using the example below, journal your feelings of gratitude, affection, and love to the most important people in your life. The next step is to tell them.

You are loved because ...

You matter to me because ...

During the courses we facilitate, the participants write positive encouraging notes to each other. They usually start like this—the woman I see in you is ...

We call these "rainy day notes" because once the course is over, they can read them again and again, especially on those "rainy days" when they are not feeling so strong or encouraged.

LYNNE'S STORY

Reconnecting—Rekindling ...

As Lynne tells us in her story, though she had held feelings of abandonment since childhood, which she re-enacted with men through various periods of her adult life, she desperately wanted to feel connected. A Blue, she longed to have an intimate relationship with a good man that would love and cherish her. As she searched deeper for a life of meaning and purpose, she was baptized into the Christian faith. She also shares that in spite of the feelings of loss and resentment in her relationship with her father; she chose to reconnect with him after a long absence.

Lynne was introduced to PIE through a business networking group. Through the feedback she received in the course, she began to recognize her leadership qualities. This was an awakening for her!

Her healing journey began with the reconnection with her dad. Then, after reflection during the course, she declared her clear intention and consciously made the decision to find that loving relationship she knew she deserved to have. She connected with a man in her singles Bible group who had joined the Army. They wrote love letters to each other while he was completing his Boot Camp. Through these letters they deepened their relationship and soon after he returned on leave, they married, with family and friends all around them. In opening and reclaiming her heart, Lynne created this amazing love story!

> Ask and it will be given to you; seek and you will find; knock and the door will be opened to you."
>
> – Matthew 7:7

Lynne's Story ...

I was born the youngest of three sisters. Because my oldest sister was born developmentally handicapped, my growing-up years were filled with turmoil. She was ten years older than me and much bigger, so I was afraid of her. Although my middle sister stood up for herself, as a little girl and the youngest in the family, I never felt brave enough to stand up for myself. I grew up resenting her because she made our home life so unpredictable and tense. I always felt like the forgotten one, as most of my mother's attention was directed towards my oldest sister. She was eventually placed in a group home facility and my mother fought for her rights in an attempt to make her life as normal as possible. She would come home to visit on weekends. This often ended with some kind of dramatic event.

I can recall feeling totally unsafe as a child. Sometimes in a rage my sister would break things, knock off somebody's glasses, or yank off my necklace. Other times she would simply refuse to go back to the group home and the police had to assist my parents in getting her back. Over the years my dad started to drink more and more. When I was in middle school my family totally fell apart and my parents got a divorce.

By the time I was in college my father was a full-blown alcoholic. My middle sister was able to reach out to my father's sister who got him help. He stopped drinking in 1991 when my aunt's husband, a psychologist, took my father to an underpass of a freeway and pointed out all the homeless people that were living there. My father realized he was one step away from this scenario for himself. My uncle told him that his daughters had one question, "Did he love them enough to get help for himself?" This was a life-changing moment for Dad. In the beginning, he started attending daily AA meetings, and has been sober ever since. That same year, my father's sister and her husband offered him a job in Hawaii. He moved, and I didn't see him again until 1997.

I had just broken off a relationship with a good Christian man, one of the healthiest I had ever had, because I was not in love with him. He and his family had introduced me to Christianity. During that relationship I made a commitment to the Lord and was born again through baptism. I now know that God's purpose was for me to marry a Christian man, and for that I am grateful. I was living in Texas at the time, so my dad flew out to take the trip to California with me in my car. I spent some quality time with him and asked a lot of questions about our past. There were so many things about our family I wanted to know. Over the twelve years we lived close to each other, I was willing to forgive him, and we started rebuilding our relationship. I also saw my father get baptized. The most rewarding time in our father-daughter relationship was last Christmas when he visited us in Germany. I watched, with such joy, my dad holding my son, his only grandson.

They say that children of alcoholics have a higher propensity to alcoholism. Without a doubt, the effects of having a father that was an alcoholic and emotionally absent during a crucial time in my life had damaged me. I felt broken. I can remember getting drunk at a party when I was 16. I cried all the way home and asked myself, "Why did my father choose alcohol over me, and why did he leave me?" I had sex for the first time at 18 with a man I thought of as my first love, my true love. His family moved away so that relationship came to an end. After that I found myself desperately looking for men to fill the dark void in my life. I felt very resentful because I believed my parents abandoned me as a little girl. The alcohol had taken over my dad's life, and my sister took over my mother's life, so where did that leave me? I remember one time in particular having sex thinking that this man couldn't possibly leave me after I gave myself to him. What a rude awakening that was! With every relationship, I was left feeling more unloved and empty, but I still continued to look for men in all the wrong places.

After many failed relationships, I was determined to seek help for my brokenness. As a family we had participated in therapy because of my sister's mental illness. I knew I had to work through my problems and feelings of inadequacy and redefine myself. Even though I had become a Christian in 1997, I was still leading a life far from God's amazing plan for me. At this point, I had a friend who introduced me to a personal development seminar. This experience was the second step in freeing me from the resentments I had towards my mother and sister. However, I never truly understood my mother until I had a child of my own. He has brought us so much closer together. I have rekindled my relationships with my family.

In 2008, through a women's networking group, I learned about PIE for women. My participation in this course was another huge turning point in my life. I started to believe I could dream big again. I was so tired of being lonely and alone. I wanted to be married to a man who would cherish and love me, for me. I desperately wanted to be in a functional, healthy marriage. In the course the facilitators talked to us about becoming the 100% person we wanted to attract in our lives. When one of the facilitators asked me, "What exactly are you waiting for?" I realized I was the only one that was holding me back from living my dream. Soon after PIE graduation I was led to the love of my life and ultimately to the most beautiful gift from God, our little boy.

During PIE I also received feedback from the other women in the course that I was a leader. They saw in me what I couldn't see in myself. This encouraged me to move forward in fulfilling my life's purpose to leave a legacy, my mark in making the world a better place. I went on to volunteer by serving on staff for the next PIE. I have had a vision from God that I would one day stand on a stage and give my testimony. By writing my story for this book, I know I am one step closer to doing just that.

I am a stay-at-home mom, the greatest career I have ever had. I am grateful to be here to witness each day of our son's life. Currently, I am going to school to be certified as a nutrition counselor. I love what I am learning for myself and my family. I look forward to coaching others. I have a real estate license and my husband and I are creating an exciting faith-based mobile application we can market together. All of this affords me the opportunity to work from home and raise our precious little son. Each day I feel more and more like the woman I believe God designed me to be.

EXERCISE – ATTITUDE OF GRATITUDE

The blessings didn't end with Lynne and Ben's love story. They now have a beautiful son. Lynne's story resonates with an attitude of gratitude, she is thankful for everything. Many days she shares her feelings of love and appreciation for her husband, son, and others on Facebook.

When you are willing to practice the 4 A's with the men in your life: Acknowledge, Accept, Affirm, and Appreciate, you will attract that which you project ("The Law of Attraction"). Simply express gratitude more often as you also lovingly and firmly ask for what you want. What women want most is to be: Understood, Respected and Listened to (URL – coined to make it easy for men to remember). Relationships are not 50-50, they are 100-100. As you bring your 100 percent into a relationship, whether it is with your husband, son, boyfriend, boss, coworker, or friend, what you project attracts the best in him. He is more likely to respond with understanding, respect, and listen to what you have to say. It starts with you!

We tell a story in PIE about the movie *As Good as It Gets*. Helen Hunt's character gets annoyed with Jack Nicholson's negativity and criticalness about everything. He has OCD and is ineffective in social situations. Moments after being seated in a fine restaurant, he told her, "They made me go out and buy a new outfit, and they let you in, in a housedress." She started to leave and said, "Pay me a compliment, Melvin, I need one, quick! A compliment is something nice you say to somebody else." The scene moves in on them, he uncomfortably shifts in his seat and finally says, "You make me want to be a better man." WOW! She acknowledges him by telling him, "It is maybe the best compliment I have ever received in my life." By using the 4 A's in your primary relationships with men, you will attract and draw the better man out of them.

What are you grateful for in your life? Who are the people that bring you joy? How do you appreciate them or yourself daily? Are you willing to openly and frequently express words of acknowledgment to others?

Are you willing to receive?

If over 80% of our thoughts are typically negative (the human condition), how do you begin to increase the good thoughts in your mind to change this statistic for yourself? First, you must be willing to bring the positive to consciousness. Just as it takes at least 24 days of focused effort to change a habit, training your brain to notice the blessings and positive things in life takes conscious practice. **The best way to kick-start this practice is at the end of each day, to write down three new things you are grateful for.** When you do this, you are forcing your brain to review good moments that happened in the last 24 hours.

As you build a gratitude list, you are developing a positive mindset and perspective on the world that counteracts the cultural bias for negativity from the news, dramatic events, and eccentric behavior of some celebrities. It does not have to be big or monumental, it could be: you found a parking space right up front today, the trash was empty when you got home, you fit into the outfit you haven't worn for a while, or you expressed thankfulness to God for your blessings and the safety of your family. As you shift your perspective and form an attitude of gratitude, you are rewiring your brain.

Gratitude Journal: I am thankful today for ...

By being thankful to others and grateful for the positive events of the day, and by acknowledging the things you've accomplished and the things you have been willing to change, you will begin to retrain your brain. This list is not repetitive; it is fresh and new every day! Writing it down affirms it twice, once in the conscious moment and again when you jot it down. You may think there is no way you can keep expanding your list, however, if you do it for at least a week and keep going, it will become a natural habit!

> I DECLARE that I will use my words to bless people. I will speak favor and victory over my family, friends, and loved ones. I will help call out their seeds of greatness by telling them 'I'm proud of you, I love you, you are amazing, you are talented, you are beautiful, you will do great things in life.' This is my declaration."
>
> – **Joel Osteen**, author, *I Declare 31 Promises to Speak over Your Life*

ELIZABETH'S STORY

Recapture—Refine ...

Elizabeth's story is truly one of victory. She was raised in affluence and influence. Her father was a self-made millionaire and respected pillar of society. As she shares her story of emotional, sexual, and verbal abuse, growing up in a wealthy family with many secrets, some might think she had it easier than most given her father's wealth.

Elizabeth is a powerful Yellow personality. She participated in one of our first PIE courses, many years ago. She was voted best leader, out of her full commitment to the process and her engaging and charismatic communication. This feedback on her leadership qualities made such an impression on her that she joined our nonprofit cause. As soon as she heard of CARTE's first mission, to provide self-esteem and personal development programs for sexually abused high-risk teens, she was on-board. She used her power and influence to raise funds for the STARR SuperCamps. In the following years, when we expanded the program to support women victims of domestic violence, she once again brought passion, connections, and contributions to make the first course possible. Her most important message to women is, "You are not what happened to you!"

Elizabeth's Story ...

> "A passionate woman who belongs to herself is irresistible."
> - Anonymous

I believe every woman carries within her the seed of greatness. For me this seed was not truly nurtured, fostered, and nourished until I became a mother. Like most life stories mine starts when I was an impressionable, innocent child, the youngest of three in a family whose social image was highly protected. Nobody knew what was happening inside the home and it was clear to all of us it was not to be discussed. I was raised in a wealthy highly respected family in an affluent area of the country. My father was president of the Chamber of Commerce and he owned a lot of real estate. He was, by all standards, a self-made millionaire and a successful pillar of society. He was also the eldest of three brothers. Their father (my grandfather) was killed by a drunk driver. I can't say for certain what happened to them as children; I will say, based on what I know today, the dysfunctional thread that ran through my father's family was sexual addiction. Once, a 12 year old male cousin of mine heard our fathers and uncle talking about the subject of how sex is great, but incest is best! My female cousins, children from my uncles, were also sexually abused by their fathers. The pain this childhood trauma caused throughout our families is still evident today, generations later.

My grandfather, my mother's father, was also a self-made millionaire. He was said to have had a large collection of pornographic material. My father who pretended to be "the great white knight" claimed to have been so disgusted by it that when it was discovered, he personally disposed of the collection. My mother had four sisters. As my mother passed away, and we never openly discussed any details of her life or my abuse, there is no way of my knowing what may have happened in her family.

Though I was quite feisty as a young girl and had a definite mind of my own, I intuitively knew how far I could go with any challenges to my father's authority. I was tall for my age and blond, so he made fun of me by treating me like a dumb blond or calling me names such as bone brain and knuckle head. Looking back, I was innately a happy little girl, but my self-esteem gradually diminished as a result of the underlying tension in the home and the events in my life. When I was 11 or 12 while being driven home by a playmate's chauffer, he reached over and put his hand between my legs. I ran inside and threw up. I told my mom and heard later that he lost his job; however, it was never discussed again.

By the time I was 16 I had forgotten the incident, I was getting good grades and I had a nice boyfriend. The night he asked me to go steady and we had our first real kiss, my father came into my bedroom and boldly stated that he would be the one to teach me about sex. He touched my body all over and told me he would be back the next night to complete his lesson. I remember feeling sick to my stomach and dirty. The next morning I told my mother the whole disgusting story and asked her to please protect me from him. I imagine she was heartsick, hearing this about my father, but it too was never mentioned again. After the incident my father never pretended to care about me. He was mean-spirited and often acted like I didn't even exist. There were so many unresolved feelings in the home, no counseling, and a lot of tension. I began to sink deeper into my feelings of inadequacy. In telling my mother, I paid a very dear price. Though the sexual abuse stopped, the verbal abuse continued and I felt emotionally distraught and abandoned.

Many years later, my sister, who is two years older than me, one day made the comment, "So you think you were the only one?" Though she has had years of therapy and has known my dedication and efforts to fund programs that interrupt the cycle of abuse, she still won't really talk about it. So we simply don't. My guess is that she, too, was sexually abused by my father and this likely protected me from further abuse. Upon reflection, when we were small children, our father would come into our rooms with a male friend to play and tickle us before bed. Recalling this still brings up uncomfortable feelings. My father's moral attitudes confused me. When he discovered that we, as children, had experimented around sex by looking at each other's genitals, he quickly told us that exploring sex with each other was dirty and would not be tolerated. Yet, there were occasions in the house when he would wear nothing but riding chaps.

After graduating high school, I went to college but I sabotaged my education. I made some very bad choices, one of which was dropping out of school and marrying a man 11 years my senior. I hardly knew him and, of course, he turned out to be very controlling, just like my father. He soon became violent and physically abusive. He attempted to choke me and more than once held a gun to my head. As he was a pilot, he decided to teach me to fly, and when I didn't do well, he threatened to throw me out of the small plane, which had a missing door. After ending up in the hospital as the result of a severe beating, I finally escaped his control through the help of a friend. I was only 22 years old, and my life was in ruins. I had allowed myself to be used sexually by men, believing that was the only way I could be loved and desired. I didn't know how to set boundaries or choose the right man for myself. I still had many lessons to learn.

I got a job with an airline and moved to the eastern part of the country where I met my second husband. At this point, I was quite immature and my self-esteem was still very low. When my aunt claimed that the man who was to become my future husband was so adorable and that if I didn't grab him right now, some other beautiful woman would, I immediately said "I do". Again, I trusted other's opinions over my own and had no concept of what was good for me.

In spite of the sexual and verbal abuse I endured as a child and the violent physical abuse I suffered in my first marriage, I wanted to become the absolute best mother I could be. The day I found out I was pregnant with my first-born, I went to the library and came home with a huge stack of parenting books on raising children with high self-esteem. This was the beginning of my intense study of self-help books. My foremost desire was to ensure the healthy development of my two sons. I was just beginning to believe in myself, as I observed my two sons flourishing. I accepted my role as a wife and mother and stayed in my unfulfilled marriage for many years. He was a loving father and my focus was on raising my sons differently than my parents had raised my sister, brother, and me. My sons excelled at everything they did—sports, school, and relationships. Their success gave me confidence as a mother, but my personal healing as a woman wasn't over.

I began to notice a pattern of disrespect from my husband towards me. He was often verbally abusive and we became incompatible sexually. Although I stayed in the marriage for 34 years, I threw myself into religion (like my mother had) and taught Sunday school and still found no peace. I was dying inside. I knew I was living a lie and not being true to me or my family, but I was also afraid of being alone and raising our boys alone. We separated once, yet ended back together because the boys missed their father, and I had so many fears. I wanted to recapture the fun-loving, feisty girl of my youth before all the layers of abuse and regrets took over my life and my mind. Then my prayers were answered, and my life began to take a much different turn.

When my oldest son graduated high school, he started dating a beautiful, bright young woman. Little did I know that relationship would be the beginning of my own personal empowerment and would completely change my life. I met the mother of my son's girlfriend, and even though our children have subsequently married others, we developed a strong friendship, which still exists today. She had cofounded a nonprofit organization called CARTE. Along with a respected therapist, they created a leadership program called PIE, in order to build leaders and mentors for STARR for at-risk teens. When she first asked me to participate in this personal-growth seminar I initially hesitated, as I thought I had already done so much work on myself, but I trusted her, so I did it.

I soon realized I had never truly seen myself as a leader. The group chose me as the best leader out of 45 participants, and I was blown away. Since my abuse, I had always been a people pleaser and from the day I graduated from PIE, I started to make choices from a position of strength. I started setting boundaries, respecting myself, and asking for respect. My husband was threatened by my empowerment and although our relationship shifted, I knew I was done with the marriage. I continued to staff these amazing seminars and also got involved with fund-raising for CARTE. I continued to grow and thrive. The leadership course was the seed, and over a number of years I embraced new opportunities for my life. My sons each married amazing women. The two families, along with my husband and I, moved out of state to follow our sons' dream to open a new business. Soon after the move my first granddaughter was born. It struck me that I had been so unhappy in my relationship for so long, I wanted to be an example of truth and strength for her; I filed for divorce after 34 years in a dysfunctional marriage. I was going to be the woman who passionately belonged to herself. I became a respected member of the community, and I was invited to participate on several nonprofit boards. My mother had passed away and then my father. My sister became the executor of their estate, which left my siblings and me financially stable. I had finally accepted living on my own, as a single woman, and I continued to grow emotionally with the support of an excellent therapist. I started to refine parts of myself once again, cultivating new friendships and joining in community with others to raise funds for women and children's programs.

Many divorced women have told me that the main reason they stayed in their dysfunctional marriages for so long is because they were afraid to be alone the rest of their lives. My friends will tell you, I was no different. After the age of 60, I often wondered who would be out there for me. I wanted to be in a healthy relationship. I had been working on myself to become a woman of excellence in all areas of my life. I totally believe in the law of attraction. In order to find the right partner for myself, I knew I had to become the person I wanted to attract. I was ready!

At age 61, a friend invited me to meet a man on a blind date. The rest is history. We are happily married today with so many things in common. We enjoy each other's company, spend as much time as possible together, and share our adorable grandchildren. I finally feel whole and cherished. Our marriage is healthy on every level. I embrace my life with my husband and know I am living the way God always intended for me. Children live what they learn; it is my belief that we need to model and teach children through our willingness to heal.

My good friend said to me recently, "What we reveal, we can heal." Those are words of wisdom. My family revealed none of the truth of our dysfunction, and never sought any outside help; as a result, there was so much unresolved pain. I have pushed myself to interrupt the cycle of abuse in my own family, and today I continue to support the personal development of abused women and teens. My goal is to be a light in the world by encouraging these victims to use the tools and principles gleaned in STARR, to build up their own self-esteem and become healthy role models for their children.

I hope and pray that my story also helps to open up the subject of abuse within wealthy families—abuse that may never otherwise be revealed. Women that come from wealth may be more hesitant to come forward. They are fearful of destroying their prestigious family images and being disenfranchised from the position, money, and status they have known. I am testimony that the truth can set us free, and that we have the power to reinvent our lives. We are not what happened to us. In healing ourselves, we are empowered to significantly interrupt the generational cycle of abuse, in our families and the world.

> Every woman who heals herself helps heal all the women who came before her and all those who will come after her."
> - Christiane Northrup, M.D.

EXERCISE – THE PURPOSE AND PASSION WITHIN

As a result of Elizabeth healing and overcoming her abusive past, she rediscovered her purpose and passion, and began paying it forward. Out of her own adversities and her willingness to stand for something, she changed the lives of many women and children. She is an inspiration, but each one of us has natural gifts and talents to contribute to our communities and the world. You have a specific purpose for being here in this world, at this time. Elizabeth found her purpose and so can you. One person can make a difference.

What breaks your heart? Is it the abusive treatment of elderly people, child abuse, someone's illness or untimely death, domestic violence, lost souls? A simple act of kindness is anything that makes a positive difference in someone else's life. The possibilities are endless, here are some examples.

Examples

- Visit an elderly person in a home where they get few visitors or little personal attention
- Connect with a women's shelter
- Coach a children's sports team
- Clean out someone's yard
- Go grocery shopping for someone who is ill
- Deliver a meal
- Encourage a hurting child or an adult
- Get involved with a nonprofit that shares your values

There are so many things you can do—and there is so much need. Write in the space below something you believe you could do, put it in your calendar, and go do it!

I commit today to ...

Random acts of kindness, volunteering, and other forms of altruism have measureable health benefits. Helping others not only gives you a greater sense of well-being, personal significance, and fulfillment in your life, it stimulates healthy responses in people observing the altruistic act.

Here is the story of how an Ohio teen, Samantha Manns, is dealing with her grief over the loss of her 89-year-old great-grandmother, who was "a really big influence" in her life. When her dearly loved great-grandmother died in February 2013, Samantha initiated a quest of performing 89 acts of kindness in her honor.

Samantha's first act of kindness was paying for the cost of the meal for the customer behind her at a drive-thru restaurant. When she repeated the same act of kindness a few days later, it set off a chain reaction, with people in turn paying for the people behind them. Samantha is also using social media to post and give suggestions for ongoing acts of kindness. Her intention is to inspire others to pay it forward. Though Samantha expects it to take about a year and a half to complete her 89 acts of kindness, she believes her great-grandmother would be proud of her.

> To paraphrase Mother Teresa, we cannot be depressed and in-service at the same time.

THE HEART IN FORGIVENESS

Life is all about relationships. The thread that runs through every story is the heart of forgiveness. In order to begin to heal and rewrite her story, each woman had to let go and make a choice to forgive—whether it was a parent, primary relationship, friend, or herself. "The Heart in Forgiveness" is a process we designed to support you in releasing childhood hurts or other disappointments, regrets, or failures, so that you can move forward in your life.

> "Forgiveness is giving up the hope that the past could have been any different." - Oprah Winfrey

When someone offends, betrays, or deceives us, it is natural to feel frustrated, angry, hurt, and resentful. Our attention and focus zeroes in on the source of our injury, and we rapidly begin building a case to justify our reaction, no matter how accurate or distorted it may be. We become driven to be right about how we view the situation, and we resist anything that doesn't support our perception. We often pay a huge price for this, sometimes destroying our relationships.

Resentments-Resistance-Revenge (Negative 3 R's) Resentments, the first of the three "Negative R's" raise their ugly head the moment we experience or perceive an injury, injustice, or conflict. We often stuff these feelings without expressing them directly to the offender in the moment. Women often tend to keep a scorecard of offenses. It is like filling a balloon, each offense fills the balloon a little more until it suddenly bursts (we lose it over some smaller offense) and our relationship is left wondering, "What just happened here?" To paraphrase something Rick Warren, pastor of Saddleback Church, said , it's always more rewarding to resolve the conflict in each moment than to dissolve the relationship.

Broken agreements often are the cause of resentments; they don't work! An agreement is between us and at least one other person. If we make an agreement, we must either follow-through or renegotiate the specifics of it (before it is broken). Repeatedly breaking agreements will eventually tear at the fabric of our relationships (especially with children). We have heard so many teens in our courses say, "I couldn't trust my parents because they would tell me they would do something, and then not do it, totally disappointing me, as if I don't matter!"

When we don't effectively communicate, our negatively charged emotions build up and we begin building a wall, which often turns into resistance, the second "Negative R." Though some of us may not have a problem confronting others, most of us don't set clear boundaries with others or define healthy expectations for ourselves. Many of us are much clearer about what we don't want, rather than what we do want. We may be vocal about our beliefs, values, and desires to others, but are either intimidated by the person who hurt or offended us or fear the consequences of telling the truth. The price of confrontation may appear so huge we take the perceived path of least resistance, inadvertently internalizing our resentments. In reality, the price of not revealing and dealing with the truth is often at tremendous physical and emotional cost to ourselves and others.

As Gloria, says, "Fear is the distance between the thought and the action." In other words, the moment we dare to take the necessary action to face our fears and resolve the conflicts that are at the cause of our resentments, our fears are usually reduced to a manageable size. The healthy way to deal with negative experiences is to set clear boundaries, hold ourselves and others accountable, and communicate honestly and respectfully when our boundaries are violated. In most situations, honest, straightforward communication usually resolves the problems. In the third "Negative R," revenge occurs when communication is compromised and there is a greater potential for loss in our relationships. We often feel obliged or compelled to do things that we don't want to do and don't feel good about doing. We then start to withhold, retreat, sabotage ourselves and others, or otherwise undermine the integrity of the relationship in one way or another, feeling altogether justified in our "sweet revenge." But the price of revenge, though it may be momentarily sweet, is ultimately toxic to our health. In the end, our resentments, our bitterness, our shame, and our guilt rob us not only of our personal power and health, but also our hope and inner peace.

When you cannot forgive others you destroy the bridge over which you too must pass. When conflicts arise we are either building a wall of resentment or a bridge of forgiveness. If we cannot forgive others, we risk not being forgiven ourselves. As none of us is perfect, at some point in our lives, we will deceive or cause injury to others and seek to be forgiven. Though it is far easier to point the finger of blame than it is to take a look at our own choices and actions—when you point outward with one finger and thumb, three fingers are pointing back at you.

Forgiveness vs. Trust

Before getting to the heart in forgiveness, it is essential to clarify what it is not. Forgiveness does not make an offender right. It doesn't mean that we immediately put our trust in the deceiver, sweep the matter under the rug, or remain in relationships that are unhealthy or abusive. In fact, there is a huge difference between forgiveness and trust. Forgiveness is a conscious choice we make in the moment. Trust must be built over time through repeatedly demonstrated positive and corrective action. Forgiveness allows us to recognize and assign appropriate responsibility where it belongs, and presents us with the opportunity to reclaim our personal power.

> Forgiveness is not a single act of courage, it is an ongoing act of grace."
> – Rose Gibbons

The act of forgiveness is the first step in the process toward healing. Too often we think it is the last step following years of working through our resentments, unyielding resistance, and letting go of bitter-sweet desires for revenge as we address our misery and pain in therapy or through self-help mechanisms. We think it is then that we are ready to forgive. In actuality, the moment we decide to forgive is the moment that all manner of healing can begin.

The 4 F's – How the Four Personalities Avoid Facing the Truth and Avoid Conflict

When we are in the "Negative 3 R's" we are avoiding dealing with our feelings in an honest and direct manner. Once we recognize the unconscious ways we avoid facing the truth about ourselves, we can consciously begin building from our strengths to initiate change, resolution, and reconciliation. Before we go to the "Positive 3 R's," we need to take a look at how each of the four innate personalities typically avoids truth and conflict when in limitations.

RED This personality is motivated by power so they tend to **fight** when in their limitations, using their power to intimidate or control the situation. However, as quickly as they explode, they are typically over it. Their strengths are that they are visionaries, directors, and natural leaders. When in fight mode they are confrontational and insensitive, and may not see or acknowledge the relationship casualties along the way. Reds are logical thinkers and task-oriented.

BLUE Blues, on the other hand, tend to **freeze** in their avoidance. They are driven by intimacy, and in their strengths, they are quality-oriented, compassionate, and committed. In their limitations, they often come off as self-righteous, and can be very judgmental and perfectionistic. This is the only personality in which they are both task and relationship-oriented. However, with a Blue, the relationship is always at the forefront—the motivating driver.

WHITE This personality is driven by peace. In their strengths they bring balance, kindness, and the voice of reason. However, in their limitations, they **faint**, disconnect, and go silent. When the pressure is high, their physical discomfort spikes. To release the pressure they typically dis-engage. Whites seek autonomy. Give them a project, instruct them in what you want them to do ... then leave them alone to do it. Whites are task-oriented, logical thinkers.

YELLOW A yellow personality most often takes **flight** (emotionally or literally) to avoid conflict. As they are driven by fun, they are usually creative, persuasive, forgiving, and engaging, but when in their limitations, they want to keep it light. When being confronted with the facts they often turn to humor to turn down the heat and distract the conversation. In their limitations they may have poor follow-through, often promising more than they deliver. Yellows are relationship-oriented.

Though we all have unique personalities, we each have an innate core color and a secondary color that express our natural strengths and limitations. We are most often held back by the limitations of our secondary color. From the "4 F's" listed above, which of these most accurately describes how you avoid facing the truth and conflict? It will either be from your motivating core color, your secondary color, or both.

The Process of Forgiveness - Recognize—Respond—Recalibrate (Positive 3 R's)

Forgiveness starts with acknowledging and reflecting on what happened to us or what we did to another. For many, this may be the toughest step as we must consciously **recognize** (the first of three "Positive R's") and confront the extent of the pain, shame, or blame that we are holding on to as a victim or an offender. Recognizing the truth gives shape, depth, and breadth to our pain and gives us a clear picture of where we are emotionally.

The next step, **respond** (the second "Positive R"), may be even more difficult for some, as it requires us to be responsible, not for someone else's behavior or the offensive act, but for how we have negatively defined and limited ourselves as a result.

In order to reclaim the personal power we gave up in defining ourselves as a victim, we must be willing to take an honest look at the debilitating choices and decisions we've made about ourselves and others. In *The Gift of Fear,* Gavin DeBecker states, "First time victim, second time volunteer." It is only through taking responsibility for our choices that we can stop being victims and begin instead to make positive adjustments in our outlook and **recalibrate** (the third "Positive R") our view of ourselves and others.

Perhaps you have been the offender and hurt someone. Unless you take personal responsibility for your actions, pay the consequences, and make amends for your behavior, you will likely live with painful regrets and unconscious guilt. This may metaphysically take the form of pain or disease. However, when you take back your power through forgiveness and make the necessary changes in harmony with your authentic self ... you begin the healing process.

The following exercise is a two-part process. In Part I, you have the opportunity to recognize the pent up feelings you have towards yourself and the offender. In Part II, you then can responsibly express what matters to you, clearly stating your intentions and expectations, and recalibrate the direction you want your relationship or your life to take.

Part I – Recognition Letter

In this exercise you are to write a letter to a person who hurt you, harmed you, or with whom you are really angry. However, it is not to be sent to him or her. It is merely for you to reflect and release negative feelings associated with the offensive behavior. For those who may have been abused and are currently experiencing considerable shame, blame, or pain, we recommend that you write this under the supervision of a life coach or therapist.

Use "I" statements, such as

I am angry with you because ...
I am hurt because ...
I am sad because ...
I am ashamed because ...
I regret ...
I am sorry for (my part in the relationship/situation, not his/her behavior) ...
The negative decisions I made about myself are ...
The unhealthy choices I made are ...

Without censoring, get in touch with the negative feelings, self-limiting thoughts, and the decisions you have made in your reaction to the offense and offensive behavior of another. If you are the one who hurt or harmed someone, broke your agreements/promises, said something hurtful in anger, or otherwise behaved offensively, it is important to express your pain, shame, guilt, and any regrets that have kept you from moving forward.

Self-forgiveness
Many of us easily forgive others. Too often, however, we are harder on ourselves. We are not self-forgiving. We think—if others really knew the things we've said and done, they too, would not forgive us. So we hide the painful truth that we alone know. We bury our shame, guilt, anger, resentments, disappointments, and regrets. And, in our unwillingness to forgive ourselves, all these negative emotions continue to hold us back and sabotage our relationships.

Use the same format to write a letter to yourself. It is an opportunity to dig deep, express, and uproot those negative feelings, taking responsibility for your part in the events, or responsibility for the choices you made about yourself and others, as a result of those events. It is time to forgive yourself. It is time to reaffirm, accept, and love yourself.

Identify your feelings

Though you are not writing a novel it is important that you use this exercise to let go of all the resentments that you have previously stuffed. What you reveal you can heal. When you are finished, you may choose to share the letter, with a trusted friend or family member, who will listen without judgment. You can also read it privately out loud in front of a mirror. A professional third party—such as a life coach or proactive therapist—may also be necessary or valuable for this purpose. When you are done writing and you are ready to let go of the negative emotions, shred the letter. The idea is to express and release, so don't keep any negative writings around to stew over.

Part II – Response Letter

Wait a few days after you have shredded the "Recognition Letter" and then write the "Response Letter," focusing on what you now want in the relationship or would have wanted from the person who hurt, harmed, or angered you (even if that person is deceased or you are no longer involved). This process has tremendous value. It releases you from the self-imposed chains of resentments, resistance, and revenge.

Begin your letter as follows

Dear (your name) and then start writing, as if you are hearing all the things you want or wanted to hear from that person and telling him/her what matters to you. Then close it with the name of the person you are referring to in this "Response Letter."

"The Heart in Forgiveness" is a process. It is a GPS tool to recalibrate and reset your course and set clear boundaries and expectations. Then, declare what you want for yourself in the present, and take the necessary actions to support it.

In all the stories you have read, all the women first recognized their limiting beliefs at some point in their stories, responded by making the necessary shifts, took positive action, and then recalibrated as needed, giving themselves forgiveness and grace.

The Value in Recalibrating ...

While change is inevitable, no one's journey is without obstacles. We will all have circumstances that may alter our course in some way, whether big or small. When we operate from a clear intention (with a target or goal) we are more likely to succeed. However, in the process, we need to recalibrate (reset our course) along the way.

To grasp the full benefit of recalibrating, we take you on a flight from Los Angeles to Hawaii, a distance of about 2,200 nautical miles. The successful timely arrival of the flight is dependent upon the interaction between the two pilots and two independent navigational systems: the Inertial Navigational System (INS) and the Global Positioning Satellite (GPS). With the expertise of the pilots and the systems in place you would think the flight would be on course, from Point A to Point B, 90-100% of the time, barring any inclement weather. In fact, to remain on course and make a timely arrival into Honolulu requires the pilots to constantly recalibrate, utilizing the independent navigational systems and the plane's instrumentation to make necessary corrections and adjustments, otherwise a mere 10° margin of error would cause the flight to miss the Islands by approximately 380 miles.

In this example, there are several valuable points to take away.

- Have an accountability partner (a copilot) in life, like a good friend who will tell you the truth, a master mind partner, or a coach that will keep you on target

- Start with a clear flight plan that identifies Point A (where you are starting from using The Pie of Life to calibrate) and Point B (where you want to be, using the exercises in the book to get there)

- Recalibrate your journey and be willing to rethink the process. In doing so, you are more likely to stay on course and achieve your goals

- Celebrate the small victories and accomplishments along the way
- Acknowledge the team of people and systems that provide a safety net of support for you (being grateful for something or to someone each day)
- Have a clear intention and develop the tools and strategies that support you on your journey. These are the keys to achieving your goals and reaching your destination—on a flight or in life

PART 3

The wisdom in rethinking your life!

The exercises, after each story in Part 2, presented opportunities for you to rethink the regrets, disappointments, and past negative events in your life that may still be holding you back. You read how each woman addressed, in one way or another, the influence and impact of her early childhood relationships with her father and mother. This was a very personal process for them, and it is likely to be for you. The exercises and journaling you have been willing to do have brought you to this point. Now it is time for you to move forward.

The next few sections are all about breakthroughs— mind, body, and spirit!

- Mindfulness (to reclaim and restore)
- Strategies for a Healthier Lifestyle (to refuel and re-energize)
- Breakthrough—Creating a Contract for Change (to recharge and renew)
- Achieving your Goals (to re-story and recalibrate)

This is rethinking your life—in action!

A MINDFUL ME IS A HEALTHY ME

Reclaim—Restore

In order to get our priorities straight so that our actions are consistent with what we say we value, it is important to understand the distinction between a self-centered focus and a selfless focus (one that empowers us to live passionately and purposefully). We often think taking care of ourselves is perceived as being selfish. To grasp the difference, once again we are going to take to the air.

When flying, many of us tend to tune out the flight attendants' preflight safety instructions about carry-on, seat belts, exit locations and oxygen masks. It is the same spiel every time. So in our courses, it never ceases to amaze us when mothers are asked, "If the oxygen mask drops down from the overhead, who do you put it on first, yourself or your child?" Many women still answer, "On my child first." The flight attendants always tell you to put the oxygen mask on you first.

Too often we are unconscious about how we sabotage ourselves and undermine our own value—at times in small ways and at other times in big ways. As parents we are willing to go to great lengths and sacrifice many things in our own lives for the sake of our children. Yet, how can we truly protect our children, impart our values, and give them the best of us if we are unconscious?

To live by our values and convictions, it is important to realize that without "oxygen", without being refueled and replenished, and without living a healthy lifestyle, we cannot fully care for our children nor model how we want them to live their lives. Putting the "oxygen mask" on ourselves first allows us to remain conscious, in the moment, and give the best of ourselves to those we love and cherish. Even if you are not a parent, how does the oxygen-mask metaphor translate into your own life? How, exactly, are you not taking care of yourself? Go back to the PIE of Life to reassess yourself in all eight categories. Recommit to improving each slice of the "PIE", one piece at a time.

In this section we introduce two simple yet dynamic relaxation and stress management daily practices that will accelerate your personal development, support you in making positive changes, and contribute to your clarity of mind and healthy well-being.

Mindfulness

> Bring Me your mind for rest and renewal. Let Me infuse My Presence into your thoughts. As your mind stops racing, your body relaxes and you regain awareness of Me.
>
> – Sarah Young, author, Jesus Calling

The first practice, mindfulness, is designed to give your mind a break, slowing it down, and quieting it to a single focus. This practice will clear your mind and focus your attention.

Mindfulness is defined in The Oxford English Dictionary as "the quality or state of being conscious or aware of something …" The English term mindfulness was used for centuries before its reference as a meditative practice. Whenever you focus your attention in one direction, while dismissing distracting thoughts, you are being mindful.

What is prayer? Intentional thoughts usually whispered or sung in mind or aloud, in ceremony, worship, intercession, celebration, plea, gratitude, sorrow, or remorse. If you have ever prayed, you have practiced a form of mindfulness.

According to a new study by Andrew Newberg, M.D., we are on the cutting edge of neuroscientific research proving a startling connection between spirituality and cognitive function. In other words, under certain circumstances, spiritual practice can make your brain dramatically more powerful. By dedicating a few minutes a day to some form of daily mindful or prayerful practice, you not only rejuvenate yourself—mind, body, and soul—you reset your internal compass.

Slowing down your mind allows you to truly focus on what matters to you. Now, you may think mindfulness is an art, or a form of meditation that requires monastic practice—a skill that most of us probably could not, do not, and will not have the patience to acquire. However, a daily habit of slowing down your thoughts, for even a short period of time, contributes not only to your healthy well-being, but your clarity of focus and purpose.

The problem is, our automatic thoughts run rampant. Produced by our unconscious mind, they trigger actions or behaviors without the involvement of our conscious mind. And our reactions to them determine our conscious thought patterns, attitudes, and behaviors. While some of our automatic thoughts are positive, the majority (about 80%) are negative. These negative thoughts sabotage our good intentions, limiting us from achieving our goals.

Unless we re-awaken our minds, being mindful of unconscious negative thoughts, and start to shift the flow of our thoughts in a positive direction, all the affirmations in our conscious-mind will not initiate the changes necessary to make some major fundamental shifts. The starting point in changing the stream of negative unconscious thoughts is a daily practice of clearing our mind.

> As Wayne Dyer, author and expert on meditation and motivation, has said, "If you change the way you look at things, the things you look at change."

Take a moment to tune into your breath and its natural ebb and flow. Notice as you breathe in, your abdominal cavity gently pushes out and your lungs just naturally fill up and expand. As you breathe out, your lungs gently collapse, pushing the air out, and your abdominal cavity constricts in a natural rhythmic motion. Some of you may think—actually my stomach doesn't go out and in when I breathe ,my chest and shoulders rise and fall. This occurs when your breathing is shallow and remains in your throat. If you look at infants and children while they sleep, you will

see their lungs expand and collapse easily and naturally
as they breathe, providing oxygen to their entire body. This is called diaphragm breathing. To gain the most benefit from any stress reducing or mindfulness exercise, it is best to breathe in this manner.

Mindfulness Exercise

Find a quiet place where you can remain without distraction or interruption for at least 10 minutes, whether inside your home or outside in nature. At this point the emphasis is on no interruptions. If you have children in your home, you may need to get up 10-15 minutes earlier than the rest of the household in order to create a peaceful environment. If you choose to sit on the floor, sit on a pillow to support your lower back. This will allow you to sit up straight. If you are sitting in a chair, sit with both feet on the floor and your back straight.

Tune into your posture such that your shoulders are level, your arms and hands are relaxed in your lap, and each vertebrae is stacked one on top of the other. Make sure your head is sitting squarely on your shoulders, and you are not nodding forward or lifting your chin up unnaturally. This straight, yet relaxed, posture allows you to remain awake and maintain an optimum mind-body connection.

If you are meditating, your eyes should be open in a soft gaze downward. When you close your eyes, it is easier to get lost in thought or fall asleep. When staring straight out, or looking around in your surroundings, it may distract you. However, those of you who may want to just tune into your environment, identify or notice one thing at a time, as if everything had a Post-it Note on it. Others may want to read devotionals or reflect on and repeat a particularly meaningful quote, verse, or poem. Still others may just want to pray. What is important here is to go to the same place daily for at least 24 days in order to allow it to become a habit. Though it is recommended that you start your day with this practice, some of you may find that 5-10 minutes behind closed doors at work during the lunch hour has a greater likelihood of producing uninterrupted, successful repetition. Whatever works for you!

Like anyone who starts meditating for the first time, you are likely to find yourself laughingly or annoyingly distracted, with racing thoughts. As you choose your experience, just notice your thoughts, acknowledge them, and then let them go. Return to your unique and natural rhythmic breath, giving yourself the grace and space to stretch your attention in 15-30 second intervals. Remember, to rewire your mind, you need to quiet your thoughts so that you can create a clear space that gives you room to fill up with positive, intention-driven meaning. Stay with it and expect laughter, impatience, and distraction. It is all part of the practice and the journey. Over time you will develop new reaffirming habits. Celebrate every second that you remain focused on your breath. And every week, add a few minutes to your quiet time. Stay with it, you will soon surprise yourself!

We recommend you keep a journal within reach, so you can write about your awareness following the process. Each session is a journey of discovery and an opportunity to quiet the mind, relax your body, to listen to your own unique rhythm, and to develop optimum mind-body connection. As you quiet the mind, you clear your head and take it off auto-pilot. It is in this mental state that you can reconsider what is important to you and, in fact, rethink your life.

Emotional Freedom Technique (EFT)

The second daily practice we recommend is EFT. Using the same energy meridians in the traditional Chinese practice of acupuncture to treat physical and emotional complaints, EFT is best described as a form of psychological acupressure. It also integrates principles of positive psychology and neuroscience, *using the tips of one's fingers to tap on several major meridians, while thinking about a specific problem and voicing a positive affirmation.* An abundance of research supports the notion that most physical symptoms can have an underlying emotional component. EFT is used to quickly reduce guilt or shame, irritating effects of a bad day, physical complaints and pain, as well as cravings. It is a practice that readily releases negative emotions, creates positive physiological changes in your body, and effectively shifts your focus.

By making it a nightly routine in the last few minutes before drifting off to sleep, you can consciously replace negative thoughts with specific, neutralizing, positive affirmations. This will effectively circumvent any resistance that you are still holding on to. You can preset your unconscious mind and body for a more relaxed sleep. As a result, you are likely to feel more refreshed in the morning.

We all have a need to be right about what we think about ourselves and others, whether good or bad. When we have negative thoughts and judgments we become emotionally congested and create energy blocks throughout our bodies. So the question to ask yourself when experiencing any noticeable pain or specific physical complaint is, "If there was an emotional reason behind the pain in my body, the congestion in my head, or my cravings, what would it be?"

Though it is recommended that you read through the entire exercise before attempting to put all the steps together, we know that some of you will jump right into the exercise to test it out. As you start tapping on the various meridian points, you may laugh and think–really, are they serious? Before you set the book aside or flip ahead, let us explain that we, too, had the same thoughts and reactions when we were first introduced to EFT several years ago. However, after practice that led to repeated beneficial results, we kept being drawn back to its value, its purpose, and its power. We then added EFT to our courses and coaching work.

EFT Exercise

Though unconsciously we all have resistance to change and letting go, EFT cuts through our resistance. It circumvents our negative beliefs, judgments, disappointments, and regrets, whether we are ready to let go or not. This is the beauty of the process! In order to return to a relaxed and balanced state, we must acknowledge our level of stress and tension. It is only then that we can neutralize the negative energy we attach to it. First, take a couple of deep breaths. Then, on a scale of 1-10 (1 being least distressing and 10 most distressing) rate the problem, complaint, or the level of your physical pain. The next step is to create your specific setup phrase.

The Setup Phrase - Every setup phrase starts in the same way and ends in the same way: Even though I have/feel ... followed by you stating your specific problem, complaint, or pain and ends with, I deeply and completely love myself. Take a look at the examples below.

- Even though I have back pain, I deeply and completely love myself.
- Even though I feel angry at my spouse, I deeply and completely love myself.
- Even though I feel frustrated with my kids, I deeply and completely love myself.
- Even though I feel irritated with my employer, I deeply and completely love myself.
- Even though I have financial problems, I deeply and completely love myself.

Now that you have developed your own setup phrase, the next step is to repeat it out loud three times while tapping continuously with 2-3 fingertips on your **Karate Point**, the edge of either hand, between the base of your little finger and your wrist (see the diagram). Follow this with a few deep breaths.

Rebalancing and Re-energizing - Next repeat the same phrase: **Even though I feel/have** (state your issue/complaint) followed by **an affirmation**, while continuing to tap with the fingers of either hand on each of the following nine energy points, starting with the eyebrow and ending with the karate point, as described and shown in the diagram. Many tapping professionals instruct you to just state the specific issue or complaint as you tap through the meridian points. We believe in order to effectively rewire your brain, and develop the optimum mindset for change, it is important you take every opportunity to circumvent any unconscious negative beliefs, judgments, and perceptions. It is just as important to repeat your self-affirming statement as you tap through the meridians.

Eyebrow (at the point where the bridge of the nose and eyebrow meet)

Side of the eye (on the bone on the outside corner of your eye)

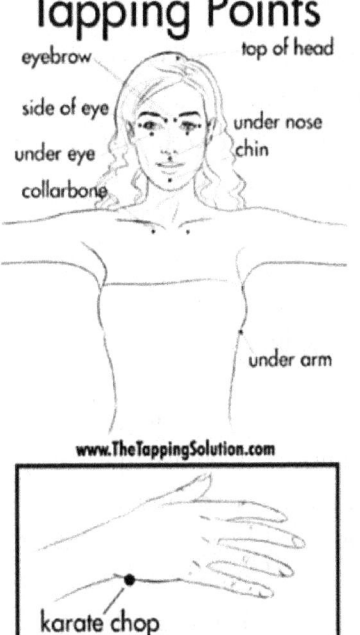

Under the eye (on bone about one inch below your eye and below your pupil)

Under the nose (midway between upper lip and nose)

Chin (midway between lower lip and point of your chin)

Collar bone (for this meridian use the tips of four fingers to tap on the area an inch or two down from and to the right or left of the 'U' at the bottom of your throat)

Under the arm (about 2-3 inches below your armpit or middle of a bra strap)

Crown (top of your head)

Karate point (the side blade of either palm of your hand midway between the base of the little finger and your wrist)

Re-assessing - Close your eyes and take a few deep breaths. Reassess how troubling or disturbing the issue/complaint is for you now, on a scale of 1-10 (10 being most distressing). Generally your level of distress drops a few levels, but does not completely disappear after a single round of tapping. Since our conscious mind tends to be stubborn and resistant to change, and our unconscious mind tends to be very literal, we usually must make re-adjustments to our original complaint/issue and our affirmation statement before completing the exercise. This can be done by adding to your original setup phrase one of the following words: **still**, **some**, and **remaining**, as in the examples below.

- Even though I still have some back pain, I accept myself. I love myself. I let go and relax.
- Even though I still feel angry at my spouse, I appreciate myself. I forgive myself. I let it go.
- Even though I still have financial problems, I love myself. I accept myself. I acknowledge myself.

Tap on each meridian point as you repeatedly state out loud your now revised phrase. Then reassess your level of stress, as you did in the first round of tapping. Although many people experience a significant decrease in negative energy after one or two rounds of tapping, some beliefs and perceptions are rather entrenched, and may need a little more work and repeated affirmation. However, this simple process should significantly reduce your level of stress, anxiety, and pain, and for some, it should completely eliminate it. www.wisdominre.org

Waiver – The publishers and authors of *RE* are not suggesting or encouraging use of EFT as a substitute for any recommended medical or mental health care. Nor are we recommending its use as an alternative to prescribed medications. If you have had some traumatic emotional experiences, whether past or present, or have serious physical symptoms it is critical for you to seek appropriate professional or medical care.

A STRATEGIC PLAN FOR A HEALTHIER LIFESTYLE

Refuel—Re-energize ...

This section covers the PHYSICAL HEALTH piece of The PIE of Life. It is all about nutrition, health, and living a healthier lifestyle. If you are committed to weight loss, it will absolutely work for you over time—assuming you follow the lifestyle plan. Intellectually, many of us know we should eat more nutritiously and exercise in order to be healthy and have energy. We've all heard that obesity and other destructive habits (like smoking) put us at higher risk for cancer, diabetes, heart disease, Alzheimer's, arthritis, sleep apnea, and other ailments. So, why aren't we all doing more to stay healthy? What is holding us back on the inside ... that may be showing up on the outside?

What is the root cause of a poor body image? Food is often a control or coping mechanism for our internal struggles. Being thin isn't necessarily a result of healthy eating. In our society, eating disorders are rampant among teenage boys and girls—from anorexia-bulimia to obesity. In fact, obesity is at an all-time high in the U.S. This is more than simply a weight issue.

> "When mind, body and spirit are in harmony, happiness is a natural state." - Deepak Chopra

So, how does a healthier lifestyle fit into your own personal-growth agenda? You have challenged yourself throughout this book, emotionally and spiritually. Now we are asking you to consider a physical challenge. Regardless of where you rated your physical health on the PIE of Life, you now have the opportunity to push yourself just a little further, by making a commitment to be healthy in mind, BODY, and spirit. To succeed, you first have to connect with the emotions that keep you from having the healthy body you say you really want. As Bobbi tells in her story, one of the most crucial reasons she didn't have the body she wanted for so long was due to her negative limiting beliefs around food and acceptance from childhood. Other women have told me that their parent's divorce, their own divorce, a significant rejection, or some other traumatic event in their lives perpetuated their spiral towards an unhealthy lifestyle. These are real issues and struggles for many women. What keeps us from being healthy, energetic, and fit today are the decisions we have made and continue to make about ourselves and our bodies, given our limiting beliefs. Today, as Bobbi shares, she is healthier and happier than she has ever been. And, the bonus is, she has an abundance of energy to achieve all her other goals and dreams.

How have your limiting beliefs distorted your vision or perception, and kept you from seeing in the mirror the woman you want to be? How have they affected your health? Allow yourself to feel those feelings. As we have said throughout this book, you have to *reveal to heal*. Take a moment for yourself to answer the following questions:

List three things you really DON'T like about your body (just three):
   1.

   2.

   3.

Go back in your memory, how old were you when you decided that you didn't like those things about yourself?

What was happening in your life at that time? (This recollection is to give you an opportunity to see the "Aha!" that may still be distracting or deterring you from living a healthy lifestyle). On a separate sheet of paper keep journaling if you need to. Then, as you've done before, shred any of the negative things you wrote in your journal and choose, once and for all, out of your own commitment to yourself, to start a 24-step challenge to a healthier, more energetic you.

In your journal or below, list five things you really love about your body? (Listing all five might be the most difficult challenge of all). Dig deep!

1.

2.

3.

4.

5.

What is your weight today? Weight _____ Date _____

In your mind, what is your ideal weight? (Make it an achievable, healthy declaration) _____

On a scale from 1-10, 10 being best, rate your current physical health overall. _____

> "When the student is ready the teacher will appear."
> - Buddhist Proverb

Are you ready to create a new exciting health story for yourself? Yes_____ No_____

I recommend you write an affirmation on a 3x5 card, reciting it in the mirror daily, "I am emotionally and physically healthy and whole" or any other "I am" statement that will move you. Every time you reach for something or do what you know is unhealthy, repeat your affirmation again and again. *It is OK to fake it until you make it.* Wear a rubber band around your wrist to remind yourself how easy it is to rubber band back to your old habits. Stretch it as a physical trigger to reset your commitment. Then, celebrate your victories daily. Repetition is the key to changing thoughts and habits.

EFT Statement - Before falling asleep or just before a meal, begin, as in the previous section (A Mindful Me is a Healthy Me), to do some deep breathing to relax yourself, and simply begin tapping on the karate chop (as shown in the diagram in the section mentioned above).

Examples -

- Even though I am overweight
- Even though I get migraine headaches
- Even though I am tired most of the time
- Even though I am kicking and screaming all the way to my health and weight goal
- Even though I have not been committed to being healthy in the past

Repeat the tapping process three times with whatever your own setup statement is and follow it up with your affirmation statement such as, "I totally and completely forgive and love myself." Then, think of three new things you are grateful for today. While you are reinforcing good healthy habits, you are retraining your brain.

I hope you choose to forge ahead with this next portion of *RE,* applying the principles to transform, refuel, and recharge your physical health. Look at the whole plan and then choose whether to apply the plan in your life, one step at a time. For successful weight loss you will need to apply all aspects of the plan. Remember, it takes up to 24 days to change a habit. - Gloria Manchester

The PIE of Health is available online at www.wisdominre.org on the resource page and is specifically designed for you to rate your health, weight, and body image today. Rate yourself on the eight steps listed on the PIE of Health (different from the PIE of Life) as you watch the video online. To gain the most benefit from this 24-step challenge you need to have a clear starting point.

Taking the 24-Step Challenge

We don't have to be stuck in our old habits! If we are willing to consciously choose new habits and are committed to doing the necessary work to retrain our brains and seek out the resources and support along the way, then we will achieve healthy results. This is the underlying premise in *RE*—mind, body, spirit transformed.

During my certification training, I simultaneously took courses with Dr. Jonny Bowden (*The Art and Science of Coaching Weight Loss*) and Dr. David Krueger (*The Neuroscience of Change*), who is also an executive mentor, coach, and Dean of Curriculum for Coach Training Alliance (where I was certificated in life-coaching).

To paraphrase Dr. Krueger, revolutionary changes in our knowledge of mind, brain, and behavior have recently come from neuroscience, psychology, quantum physics, and mindfulness practices. The application of these disciplines with strategic coaching can help you become significantly more effective in all areas of your life. Our brains ... are not fixed, but are changeable. We can rewire our brains to change habits and create new stories.

Applying the strategies from each of the two disciplines, I was determined to pass them on to anyone who would listen. I continued to teach everything I learned to my coaching clients, family, and friends. Most responded favorably, telling me they knew they should focus on their health, eating more nutritionally and exercising; they just hadn't done it. It takes conscious commitment, support, and accountability to get and stay healthy.

According to Adele Davis, nutritionist and author of *Optimum Health*, "The way I see it, every day you do one of two things—build health or produce disease in yourself."

If it was easy to make a permanent healthy lifestyle shift you would have done it by now! I think Rose's story of her New York Minute proves that if you don't have your breath and your health—nothing else really matters. When she got ill, as she tells us in her story, she was living a healthy vibrant California lifestyle. That had everything to do with her miraculous recovery. When you put the "oxygen mask" on yourself first, you can then care for your family and others who need you, accomplish your goals and live out your dreams. It takes energy to make great things happen! This is all about refueling your body and re-energizing yourself.

You may have other reasons to go through this section. Perhaps you have to lose some weight to regulate diabetes. You may or may not be overweight but you need to lower your cholesterol. You may have an auto-immune or other debilitating disease and want to reduce some of the physical pain you are experiencing. I am 67 and have Rheumatoid Arthritis. To live out my dreams of successfully building and managing my businesses, keeping up with and caring for my grandchildren, traveling, writing, facilitating courses, coaching, and continuing to make a positive difference in others' lives—*it is essential I stay healthy and full of energy.*

For several years, I had been holding on to my last 10-15 lbs. always claiming I could take it off anytime I chose to. While that was true, I did not do it. I realized it was an excuse. I had to shift that negative, self-defeating thinking to make it happen. To succeed, I consciously made a committed choice and was willing to be supported and held accountable in coaching. During my nutritional coach training, I set a personal weight goal to reach by my birthday in 2012. I can honestly state that I reached my goal and I am still right on target almost a year later.

Just like everything else Rose and I have written to encourage and support you in successfully changing something in your life, it all starts with your commitment to form a new habit. If you want to lose weight in a safe, effective manner (not quick weight loss) or get healthier this program will motivate you in rewriting that part of your story. I am providing a plan you can work on your own. Keep in mind, however, there is plenty of evidence that any plan is significantly more effective combined with a strategic coaching model and/or accountability partner.

As you have read, when we started to write this book, Rose got extremely ill and almost died. This happened shortly after I had reached my weight goal. At one point, her weight plummeted by 15 lbs. over a short period of time. I decided this was my opportunity to really use what I had learned. My overall goal was for everyone in my life to experience the energy and joy of healthy living. Rose needed to be brought back to her normal weight and be in good health. I planned a nutritionally sound menu for her while she was in the nursing facility for two weeks (bringing the food into the facility) and continued when she came to stay with me at my home. I had to bring her back to a healthy weight, eating the same foods I was eating, and not gain any weight myself. Well, an extra two Ensure milkshakes a day made with bananas, blueberries, and almond butter for Rose was our winning formula, and we did it!

Feed your body right, and you won't crave junk foods. Our bodies are made to digest natural whole foods. We are meant to eat slowly and consciously, not on the run, in front of a computer, or while watching TV. Many are following the Standard American Diet (SAD). Is this a good thing? Not really. The majority of America is eating a lot of processed foods, which have been found to prompt the build-up of toxins in our system and keep us addicted to unhealthy carbs. When we consume processed food that is so full of toxins, it is actually amazing that our bodies don't just shut down. This is why obesity is such a huge problem in the U.S. today. I believe we need to stay educated by reading labels for grams of fiber, fat/sugar content, unhealthy oils, bad carbs, and preservatives.

I am a foodie! I had been cooking fresh and fairly healthfully for a few years prior to my nutrition course, but I was still holding on to those few pounds. I have co-written a cookbook, taken cooking classes from a recognized school in Florence, Italy, and studied cooking techniques for several years on food network shows. My nutritional coaching course was quite complex: we read and discussed several books on food production, dieting, metabolic balance, fat burning, stress, sleep, exercise, food supplements, and so on. Though tremendously informative, it was a major time commitment, quite costly, and really designed to coach others on weight loss.

I have integrated the principles I learned from the experts in neuroscience and nutrition, and my own practices to give you a sensible and simple 24-step plan that isn't highly regimented (no daily recipes, weighing of foods, or stringent eating plan to follow). However, you must bring your commitment to the table. On the front end, it may look quite challenging, as it could be a substantial lifestyle shift for some of you.

You can do it one step at a time ... until "suddenly" your weight begins to drop off or level off and your energy begins to soar! Check off three or four items listed (hydration should always be first) to start the plan, incorporating other items, adding a little more movement as you go along. It is my goal to have you fall in love with healthy natural foods and with movement (notice I didn't say exercise). I call this plan a natural health regimen for contemporary living.

Here's my 24-Step Challenge for Wellness and Weight-Management

1. **Drink water** - half your weight in ounces daily (if you weigh 140 lbs. drink 70 oz per day). Dr. Bowden suggests drinking a bottle of water (approximately 16 oz) 20 minutes before eating. Sufficient water intake is a must-do. For my Canadian and European readers, you will have to recalculate in kg.
2. **Begin eliminating most processed/refined foods** like fried foods, potato chips, commercial pizza, cake, cookies, candy, canned

goods. You know what it is for you. If you are working on losing weight you will need to eventually eliminate 90% of all unhealthy carbs.
3. **Always eat breakfast** that includes a healthy carb and a protein.
4. **Eat healthy carbs** like oatmeal for cereal with almonds; most fruits such as grapefruit, berries, apples, pears and all vegetables (especially green ones) except corn and potatoes.
5. **Every meal should include at least one protein** (stimulates your metabolism and makes you feel FULL), a healthy carb and a healthy fat (avocado, olive oil, foods with Omega3). Do not sit or sleep right after eating. Take a walk or simply move around in some way.
6. **Eat something healthful about every three hours.** Bring pre-packaged snacks like almonds and toasted pumpkin seeds to work with you.
7. **Eliminate all refined oils and margarine from your pantry.** Replace with "good fats" like pure extra virgin olive oil (EVOO), coconut oil, or nut oil. Use unsalted butter in limited amounts for flavor.
8. **Plan a weekly menu.** Shop for fresh produce and other fresh food once a week. Buy in smaller quantities, knowing what you are going to be cooking, before going to the store.
9. **Eat vegetables/salads daily** with a protein and a "good fat". Choose one green vegetable every day. Consider making your own dressings. It takes five minutes or so to do, and making your own is the only way you can control the good fat content with no preservatives. Keep everything crisp. Recipes will be online.
10. **Wash and dry your vegetables** thoroughly when purchased and use "green bags" or other fresh produce bags to store them. They will keep longer and fresher.
11. **Eat lean red meat sparingly.** Exchange ground beef recipes for ground turkey, eat skinless chicken, lean pork tenderloin, or fish, as often as possible. Remember eggs are a good source of protein.
12. **Eat only whole grain breads** with a minimum of three (3) grams of fiber; if you are allergic to wheat, then use only gluten-free breads and flour.

13. **Introduce yourself to Quinoa** (pronounced keenwa), one of the super foods. Quinoa provides valuable amounts of heart-healthy fats, vegetable protein, and small amounts of the Omega-3 fatty acid.
14. **Eliminate** white rice and white pasta. Wheat pastas and brown rice are much more flavorful and Quinoa can be a healthy replacement for rice and pasta.
15. **Slowly begin** to exchange sodas (diet and non-diet) with caffeine-free green tea or a low sugar fruit juice mixed with 1/3 water.
16. **Substantially reduce your sugar** intake overall. 4.2 grams equals 1 tsp. of sugar. Read labels for grams of sugar. It is in almost everything that is processed.
17. **Take food supplements** daily, especially Vitamin D, Calcium, and Omega 3, fish oil, as well as multi-vitamins and minerals.
18. **Wear a step monitor** to reach 8,000-10,000 steps (measures lower body movement of any kind) at least four days a week, moving your body after every meal including dinner. You may also want to add some stretches and strength training. It is all about metabolic rate. Metabolism is a collection of chemical reactions that takes place in the body's cells. It converts the fuel in the food we eat into the energy needed to power everything we do, from moving to thinking.
19. **Weigh yourself once or twice weekly** (if you are managing weight loss) to make sure you are on the right track. Journal your weight and also your energy levels on a scale from 1-10, with 10 being "I feel great".
20. **Keep a food diary** for the first 24 days until you have formed new habits.
21. **Stay conscious while eating.** Make a commitment today—mindful eating is the key here. Don't eat while watching TV, at the computer, or standing.
22. **Use an affirmation like** "I am more energized and healthier with each new day". Say to yourself daily whatever makes you see the picture of a healthier you.
23. **Often when we feel stressed,** out of control, or out of balance, depression can follow. Stress and depression cause us to eat and

gain weight. See previous section for stress reducing meditations.
24. **Get a sufficient amount of sleep.** Study after study tells us that sleeplessness contributes to weight gain and stress. While sleeping your body is regenerating.

Note - To totally support your success, consider participating in a professional accountability group like HEALS www.wisdominre.org/resources.

> "Money is a result, wealth is a result, health is a result, illness is a result, your weight is a result—we live in a world of cause and effect."
> -T. Harv Eker, author

HEALS—Health, Energy, Accountability, and Lifestyle Shifts – is designed as a strategic coaching webinar series to support participants in getting healthy and fit, from the inside out. HEALS is about breaking through the barriers that have been holding you back from having the healthy body you say you want. In this series, you will be empowered to maintain a healthy weight by learning sound nutritional information, meditation, and exercises. Coaching is a very affordable gift you give yourself.

Setting a health goal - You must keep the goal in full view every day, in order to succeed in your weight loss and overall health goal. As described in Part 2 with the financial goal, when you write out your goal, it becomes more tangible, reaffirming your intention.

A SMART Goal stands for **Specific** (a clear and focused intention), **Measureable** (it has a start and ending), **Achievable** (it is not just a nice idea), **Risk** (it stretches you beyond your comfort zone), and it has a **Timeline** (a specific date by which you will complete it).

Example of a SMART GOAL- To weigh a healthy 130 lbs. by following the 24-step plan and enthusiastically move and exercise daily by 3/31/13.

Potential Barrier - Negative self-talk

Steps - To achieve your goal, I recommend you create at least 10 steps, selecting some of them that would be helpful to you, from the 24-step plan provided.

Example of an Affirmation - "I am emotionally and physically healthy and whole."

Retraining Your Brain

You can retrain your brain to accept your healthy new habits, by using this four-part process (goal, potential barrier, 10 steps, and affirmation). Write it all on a poster, placing it in full view daily. My poster is right behind my computer monitor, where I look up at it many times a day and Bobbi's is in her gym, where she works out every day.

> After smoking for 18 years, I can now say I am smoke-free. I also reduced my weight during the health and nutrition webinar series. By participating in HEALS, I learned more about meditation, EFT, nutrition, and exercise, with the accountability and support of the coaches, Gloria and Bobbi, and the other women on the HEALS team with me. I am really proud of myself. I have maintained a healthier lifestyle and I will continue with even greater motivation and determination to fulfill all my personal goals."
>
> - Carla, graduate of PIE and HEALS

BREAKDOWN-BREAKTHROUGH

Recharge—Renew ...

Our work with women and teen girls can be capsulized in this one concept, breakdown-breakthrough. To the degree you are willing to "take a look" (reflect) and tell yourself the truth about what's working and what's not working (rethink) in your life, you will achieve a corresponding breakthrough. The truth shall set you free, but first it might piss you off. In completing the exercises throughout *RE*, you have made some discoveries about yourself. Some of these may have been good, or not. Taking responsibility for your feelings, thoughts, and actions with forgiveness and grace, rather than blaming or shaming is a growth process. It takes practice, determination, and at times, courage. It will pay off! To transform from a caterpillar to a butterfly requires what we described in the LEAP Winning Results Chart™—commitment, excellence, and being open to change and opportunity.

In this section we introduce a personal declaration statement, a contract with yourself for yourself. It serves to support you in the re-story of your life! It is a short "I am" statement that speaks to the woman you are striving to become.

In your comprehensive Color Code profile is a list of your natural strengths and limitations. Choose at least three strengths from your innate color and then one or two from any of the other colors on your chart. Although they are natural strengths, you may have been struggling with some of them, or not using them to your full advantage. If you have not taken the full comprehensive yet, you can go to www.wisdominre.org/colorcode. Though the cost is $30, net proceeds are used to support the CARTE self-esteem programs for disadvantaged teens and women.

Creating Your Contract for Change

Examples - If you are timid (a White limitation), you may want to be more bold (a Red strength) or engaging (a Yellow strength). If you are overly cautious and perhaps don't take enough risks (a Blue limitation), you may want to be more spontaneous (a Yellow strength). If you have a need to be right and are argumentative (a Red limitation), you may want to be more empathic or compassionate (Blue strengths). If you often don't follow through with what you say you will do (a Yellow limitation), you may want to use the word determined (a Red strength). If you tend to power your way through situations (a Red limitation), you may need to learn to be more kind and tolerant (White strengths).

In other words, you want to develop effective traits that counter your limitations. If you are a Yellow, for example, you probably don't need fun-loving in your contract because that is your driving motive. From the following list, choose eight traits that you desire to develop and write them in the space provided.

Abundant	Accepting	Accountable	Ambitious	Appreciative	Authentic	Balanced	
Beautiful	Bold	Brave	Caring	Centered	Charismatic	Committed	
Compassionate	Confident	Contributing	Courageous	Creative	Decisive	Deserving	
Determined	Discerning	Empathic	Empowered	Empowering	Energetic	Engaging	
Expressive	Fit	Flexible	Focused	Forgiving	Fun-loving	Grateful	
Healthy	Honest	Intuitive	Kind	Loving	Mindful	Open	
Passionate	Peaceful	Persistent	Powerful	Resilient	Resourceful	Respected	
Risking	Self-assured	Self-loving	Spontaneous	Tender	Tolerant	Transparent	
Trusting	Trustworthy	Valued	Victorious	Visionary	Whole	Worthy	

Read through the entire list before deciding what traits you want to develop in yourself.

1.

2.

3.

4.

5.

6.

7.

8.

Now narrow it down to three and add the "I AM" ending with "woman". The "I AM" is present tense; it is personal and a powerful affirmation of the woman you aspire to be. As you digest your new contract, it will begin to resonate with you and others. Remember, it takes 24 days to form a new habit so make it a daily declaration. Say it to yourself in the mirror in the morning, right in the middle of your daily challenges, and always just before bed. You will be resetting your unconscious mind to a powerful declaration of the woman you want to be.

Your new contract (statement of declaration) is:

I am a _____, _____

and _____ woman.

Now, regardless of what you think it should be, before you accept it as a final contract, it is always good to ask a close and trusted friend, "Do you think I need to be more _____?" (using one of the traits here that you think you need to have in your contract). Your friends might say, "I think you are already that", then you can go back to the drawing board. Or, just check with a few more people close to you asking, "What do YOU think I need to learn?" If two or more tell you the same thing ... rethink. It is feedback!

Below are examples of contracts for the four different personalities

RED	I am an accepting, peaceful, and valued woman.
BLUE	I am a forgiving, self-assured, and spontaneous woman.
WHITE	I am a trusting, engaging, and expressive woman.
YELLOW	I am a determined, focused, and mindful woman.

Put your final contract on 3x5 cards; sign your name and date it. Put them all over the place—in your wallet, on your bathroom mirror, where you work out, everywhere. Practice, practice, practice. It is absolutely OK to fake it until you make it!

> Whatever follows the 'I am' will come looking for you."
> - Pastor Joel Osteen

We all have barriers to success. Our limitations are those barriers, and often show up as the limitations in our secondary color. If you have done the comprehensive color code, select three limitations from your list (at least one from your secondary color). What negative traits might get in your way of becoming the woman you aspire to be?

My barriers to successfully living out my contract (personal declaration) are _____, _____, _____.

Now be mindful of the one barrier that comes up for you most often. Check in with yourself, and if that limitation is holding you back, then make the necessary shift. Again, use the LEAP Playing to Win™ Chart to recalibrate.

Boundaries

What is a boundary? To paraphrase Dr. Henry Cloud and Dr. John Townsend in the book, *Boundaries: When to Say Yes and When to Say No to Take Control of Your Life*, in large measure, boundaries define us—they define what is me, and what is not me. A boundary shows me where I end and where someone else begins. When we have clear boundaries we take ownership of our own thoughts and feelings and not someone else's. While it is easier to determine a physical boundary, like a property line, many of us struggle to set and maintain boundaries in our relationships. Those who have a tendency to be codependent often enable others. Instead of being honest and sharing their own authentic thoughts and feelings, they protect the feelings of others by telling them what they think they want to hear, most often to avoid conflict.

We can only take responsibility for our own perceptions and feelings. When we attempt to control another's, we end up conflicted and confused, and so do they. They don't really know what we're asking of them. To paraphrase Dr. Cloud, you know you are codependent when you are dying and someone else's life is flashing in front of you. This, of course, is an exaggeration of how a codependent thinks. It is most often about a need to control, and it is always unhealthy.

There is so much more to boundaries, communication, and goal-setting. You are more likely to learn to set boundaries, communicate more effectively, and achieve your goals with the support and accountability of a life coach.

ACHIEVING YOUR GOALS AND LIVING YOUR DREAMS

> "What would you dream and achieve if you believed you could not fail?"
> - Inspired by Robert Schuller, pastor and author

Re-story—Recalibrate

Partner in Excellence is not called Partner in Mediocrity for a reason. Our courses are all about transforming your life, living in excellence, and developing yourself into the woman of your dreams. This happens in stages much like the caterpillar transforming itself into a butterfly. **Is it time for you to stand up in this world**, stand in excellence, and be counted? To achieve the significance and success you seek you must declare, "I matter and I am here for a purpose greater than myself." *When you stand for nothing, you fall for anything.* When you take a stand, as Elizabeth did for abused women and kids, or as Lynne did in finding a "good man" who would love and cherish her for who she is— that's standing for something! *Elizabeth writes in her story what she discovered, a passionate woman who belongs to herself is irresistible.*

When did you stop dreaming big? When did you start settling, lowering the bar of expectations for your life? When did you give up your desire to excel in all areas of your life? What is it you want that you have not already gotten or experienced? It could be a healthy relationship, a home, a functioning family, travel, a new career, and so on. You choose!

The first step in the transformation process is the "caterpillar stage." As we have described in various ways, we are born with a unique innate personality that comes with specific natural strengths and limitations. In order to build on your strengths, you must embrace all of who you are authentically (your innate core color).

The second step in the process of personal growth is the "chrysalis stage" in which you begin to develop trust in yourself, as you reflect and re-assess your life. It's at this point you ask yourself, "What's working and what's not working?" and begin to make different choices. Keep what is working, rethink what is not, and begin to take bold action to make necessary, positive changes.

Albert Einstein said, "Insanity is doing the same thing, over and over again, and expecting different results." This book, the exercises, and The Color Code are now tools in your results-oriented strategy for success. If something is not working, shift! Do something different. Use the Playing to Win Chart to help you recalibrate along the way.

The next question to ask is, "Who was I born to become?" You were designed to be a butterfly, designed to fly! If you recall in Gloria's story, as long as she held on to being her father's son, she wasn't fully living in her own design. You are unique, now be authentic. Once again, as Dr. Hartman in *Color Your Future* says, "Heed that music inside of you, no one else hears it exactly the way you do!"

The last stage of transformation is the "butterfly stage." As you free yourself of the limitations that have been holding you back, and build on your own strengths, and those of other colors, you free yourself to become who you were authentically meant to be. It is then that you find your purpose, passion, and significance.

> How does one become a butterfly? First, you must want to fly so much that you are willing to give up being a caterpillar."
> - Trina Paulus, author, *Hope for the Flowers*

Are you ready to let go of the disappointments and regrets that have been holding you back? Are you ready to make a shift in your perceptions of yourself? Are you ready for a breakthrough? Though there is no magic wand, the next exercise will support you in getting what you say you want.

Dream Letter – The Re-Story

The Dream Letter is all about visualizing and imagining yourself living the best life possible, within the next 12 months.

>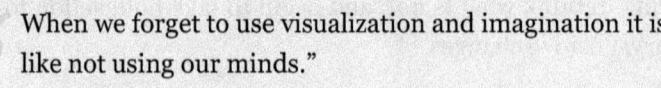
> "When we forget to use visualization and imagination it is like not using our minds."
>
> - Jose Silva, author

Type or write your letter as if you have already accomplished all the things you describe. You won't be shredding this one—it is designed to re-inspire you to take action. At the start, date your letter 12 months from now. Dream big, writing down all the things you want to "be-do-have" in the next 12 months (as if you have already accomplished all of them).

Below is an example of how to start your letter:

Dear _____,

After completing *RE* and the exercises, I had an opportunity to re-assess my life, rethink what was not working, and re-affirm what was working at the time. Then I began to dream big with intentionality, action, and accountability. I am now living my dreams. Low scores in the pieces of my "PIE of Life" improved significantly in the following areas (see examples of the eight pieces of the PIE below):

- Emotional health
- Finances and career
- Relationships
- Service/community
- Spirituality/meditation
- Fun, recreation and travel
- Physical health

By writing down the specific goals and dreams that you will attain over the next year, as if you have already accomplished them, and by rereading this letter often to stay on track, you will retrain your brain to think through and stay focused on what you want to achieve. It will open up opportunities and possibilities like never before.

> Writing this letter to myself was very powerful for me. In a new and different way, I visualized my true professional and personal goals and came up with a plan on how I would get there. It also narrowed and prioritized the unorganized thoughts that were in my mind. By spotlighting the important areas of my life, my career, marriage, and family relationships, they all improved. Thank you for this amazing opportunity."
>
> - Jaime Bongiorno Deyarmin, PIE graduate

As you make positive changes in your life, you will come up against opposition and resistance. It may be from your significant other, children, family, friends, coworkers, or your own self-sabotage. We all have a fear of change. It is the human condition.

In the courses we tell a story about crabs. A woman walks into a store in New Orleans and sees some crabs swimming in a very shallow pan. She asks the storekeeper, "Aren't you afraid some of the crabs may get out of that shallow pan?" He answers, "No ma'am, as soon as one tries to get out, the others will just pull it back in."

As you transform parts of your life, be mindful of the crabs that may want to pull you back in, including yourself. As you make changes the people in your life may get scared. They could be afraid that you will leave them behind as you grow. And, perhaps you're afraid of leaving others behind. Though your mind has been stretched, those around you have not necessarily had the same experience. You will need to be patient and loving, and still be true to yourself. That's the victory and that's the win-win.

> "A mind that is stretched by a new experience can never go back to its old dimensions."
>
> - Oliver Wendell-Holmes Jr.

Use the LEAP Playing to Win™ Chart to recalibrate whenever necessary. Be discerning and stay strong in your choices around becoming a healthier you. Nobody lives your life for you. Again, as Dr. Hartman says, "Heed that music inside of you, no one else hears it exactly the way you do!" You are unique, capable, and enough. Now go out in the world and be authentically you!

ABOUT

The wisdom in rethinking your life!

ALL ABOUT CARTE, INC.

(Child Abuse Resolved through Education)

"Rethinking Community"

> "All it would take for the forces of evil to conquer the world ... is for a few good women to do nothing."
> - Inspired by Edmund Burke who was an Irish statesman and wrote a version of this in the late 1700's.

This quote is as real today as it was in the late 1700's. "Rethinking Community" is about standing up for our beliefs and having the courage and conviction to take action in some way. Our work with *RE*, PIE, and STARR is about strengthening women and developing leaders. **We believe that women are the tipping point of peace and prosperity in the world today.**

If all of us strived to create more peace within ourselves, free from disappointment and regret, how would that translate to our families and our communities? In 1990, out of the personal commitment of a small group of women in business, we founded the 501 (c) (3) nonprofit, CARTE, INC. (Child Abuse Resolved through Education), and STARR- Succeed through Accountable Responsible Resolve, to provide self-esteem programs for an under served population of teens and women. The force of evil in the world, for us, was the issue of generational child abuse. As we came together as leaders, we discovered that out of eleven women, seven had been sexually abused or violated in some way during their childhood. This was our inspiration to begin the work of building-up teen girls and women.

When you purchase *RE*, The Color Code, or participate in PIE or LEAP to Excellence corporate workshops, and personal/professional coaching, you are not only improving yourself, you are also taking a stand for something greater than yourself. Net proceeds from all these programs provide self-esteem programs for underprivileged women and teen girls. It is a win/win.

CARTE's Vision and Mission Statement

CARTE's vision is to be a bold interruption in the cycle of domestic violence, abuse, and exploitation of children. Through our dynamic, committed leadership, our ultimate mission is to champion women and teenage girls who have experienced abuse—inspiring and encouraging them to strive for excellence, through their courageous participation in the programs offered by CARTE.

The CARTE STARR Program is an accelerated, experiential, six-day self-esteem STARR SuperCamp specifically designed for high-risk teens and victims of domestic violence. This program is a bold and dynamic intervention for healing the wounds of abuse. It inspires and encourages the participants to redefine themselves (they are not what happened to them) and to take positive action in their lives. STARR stands for Succeed through Accountable, Responsible Resolve.

CARTE's nonprofit story is about a girl who, as she is walking along the beach, picks up one starfish and throws it back into the ocean. A man comes along and asks, "Why are you doing that, there are tens of thousands of starfish that have washed ashore and will die, what possible difference can you make?" The girl picked up another starfish and as she threw it back into the water she said, "It makes a difference to this one."

In today's technological world, the girl goes to the ocean with her cell phone, blasts a post or tweet to all her friends, to send to their friends, inviting them to come and help her save thousands of starfish. A single message goes viral! That's what we can do with *RE*. We hope you will share this book with your family and friends, rethinking your community. www.starrpartners.org

Fearless Parent - As parents we often need assurance that we are doing everything possible to protect our children from internet abuse, abduction, bullying, and all forms of abuse and violence. We all want to raise healthy, emotionally intelligent children armed with self-confidence and self-esteem. At times this can be a daunting task.

By becoming an educated, empowered Fearless Parent™ you can predict, protect, prevent, and proactively maintain the safety of your children. A well-informed and equipped parent can significantly reduce the potential for abuse of their child. Through a live webinar series we are bringing parents together to discuss and resolve many of these issues.

www.myfearlessparents.com

Cooking for the Soul
This is our newest fund-raiser. It will be an online cookbook that involves a therapeutic process, in community with others, while eating healthy delicious foods you make together. Look for it soon!

www.wisdominre.org/resources

The Board of Directors and volunteers of CARTE, and our main corporate partner, LEAP want to thank you for contributing to our mission and using *RE* to support your recommitment to your own goals and dreams. As a result of the success of this book, we will fund and produce another STARR SuperCamp for at-risk teens.

www.starrpartners.org

ALL ABOUT LEADERSHIP EDUCATION ACTION PROGRAMS (LEAP)
(Corporate Sponsor for CARTE)

Partner in Excellence (PIE) Personal Development Course and Retreat

PIE is a two-day experiential course and retreat for women who want to recharge and renew their lives. The women who wrote their scars-to-stars stories in the book made real-life shifts through their full participation in PIE. *RE* is an introduction to this coursework and a powerful beginning for you. To continue your personal-growth in a safe, supportive, and dynamic group environment, we encourage you to enroll in the next PIE nearest you www.leaptoexcellence.com/pie

The LEAP-STARR Course for Teen Girls

An exciting two-day course specifically designed to launch young women, ages 14-18, on a journey to discover their true identity and purpose. STARR stands for Succeed through Accountable Responsible Resolve. In a safe and pro-active environment, with music and exercises, they learn to ...

- Communicate more effectively
- Give and receive honest feedback
- Develop healthy boundaries and keep themselves safe
- Build their self-esteem and confidence
- Connect and build a safety net of support
- Commit to their hopes and dreams
- Break through their limitations

With the technological world as it is today, our teens are facing challenges that no generation prior has ever experienced. As parents, we all want to raise emotionally healthy children and at times ,this can be very difficult. STARR for teens teaches the girls the same principles of success that are described throughout *RE*. www.leaptoexcellence.com

LEAP and LEAD to Excellence Workshops for Professionals

thrive IN THE NEW WORLD ECONOMY

The LEAP and LEAD to Excellence Workshops are two dynamic ways in which companies are building stronger, more effective teams. These teams not only make a significantly greater contribution to corporate goals and objectives, they attain individual performance objectives as well. By participating in these accelerated one-day trainings, that include 30 and 90 day webinar follow ups, your team will not only exponentially increase their professional potential, the value and benefits gained will translate into personal accomplishments. Most corporate trainings do not recognize the importance of focusing on both professional and personal development in order to establish a win/win culture. The key to thriving in this economy is to develop people. For more details go to www.leaptoexcellence.com

HEALS—Health, Energy, Accountability, and Lifestyle Shifts

HEALS is designed as a strategic coaching webinar series to support participants in getting healthy and fit, from the inside out. HEALS is about you breaking through the barriers that have been holding you back from having the healthy body you say you want. The webinar series provides sound nutritional information, exercises, and meditations that will totally support you in shifting your unhealthy habits. Nutritional group coaching is a very affordable gift you give yourself. A coach empowers you, and holds you accountable, giving you the support and encouragement you need to follow-through in reaching your healthy goal weight. Go to www.leaptoexcellence.com/leap-heals-program

> I went to PIE for women in 2010 and recently participated in the HEALS Weight and Health Management Teleseminar with Gloria Manchester and Bobbi DiClaudio. One of the main reasons I signed up for HEALS was to gain control in reducing my high cholesterol and triglycerides. I am happy to say that in only four weeks of following the program my triglycerides went from 489 to 119 and my bad cholesterol (LDL) went from immeasurable to 109. Before HEALS, I was a fairly healthy eater and doing water aerobics three to four times a week. I found out through my full participation in the HEALS class that unless I worked through my health and body image, from the inside out, mind, body, and soul, I would not experience the permanent results I was seeking for so long. I learned a little more about nutrition and exercise and a lot more about meditation and about myself. My affirmation now resonates with me, "I am a healthy, self-accepting, engaging, and confident woman."
>
> - Testimony from Judi VanKirk

LEAP Personal and Professional Coaching

LEAP offers accountability group teleseminars, emotional-intelligence, lifestyle and nutritional coaching for corporate teams, small business owners, and entrepreneurs, as well as women and teens. Are you ready to take the LEAP today to transform your life! Go to www.leaptoexcellence.com and go to the page on personal and executive coaching to register for one of our innovative coaching webinars or workshops.

Exclusive Image

Like many businesses, Jeff Murphy's company was borne out of his desire to differentiate himself from the status quo. His professional goal is to offer excellence in customer care, along with outstanding graphic services to meet each client's requirements and budget. From logos, templates, websites, and promotional products, Jeff understands a successful design is more than just pretty artwork. His amazing talent is evident as you look throughout *RE*. www.exclusiveimage.net

RETHINKING AND JOURNALING

NOTES

PART 1

1. *Criminal Minds: The Slave of Duty (#5.10)*, CBS (Agent David Rossi to Prentiss).

2. *Wisconsin Council on Children and Families*, winter 2007, Vol. 1, www.wccf.org/pdf/brain_dev_and_early_learning.pdf,

3. Bruce Lipton, *Biology of Belief - Unleashing the Power of Consciousness, Matter & Miracles*, Hay House Publication, 2008.

4. Shawn Achor, *The Happiness Advantage*, Crown Publishing Group, 2010.

5. Taylor Hartman, *Color Code Personality Profile*, www.colorcode.com

6. Taylor Hartman, *The People Code: It's All About Your Innate Motive*, Scribner 2007.

7. Rick Warren, *Purpose Driven Life – What on Earth am I Here For?*, Zondervan, 2002.

8. Rick Warren, *Start the Healing by Revealing the Hurt*, Daily Hope Devotional, July 27, 2012.

9. Henry Cloud, Ph.D. & John Townsend, Ph.D., *Boundaries: When to Say Yes and When to Say No*, Zondervan, 2008.

10. John C. Maxwell, *Developing The Leader Within You*, Nashville, Thomas Nelson Publishers, 1993 pgs. 62-63.

11. Earl Nightingale, *Lead the Field*, Simon & Schuster Audio/Nightingale-Conant, February 2002.

12. *Oprah's Life Class with Anthony Robbins*, www.oprah.com/oprahs-lifeclass, April 2, 2012.

13. Adelle Davis, *Let's Eat Right to Keep Fit*, Harcourt, Brace, Jovanovich, New American, 1970.

14. Aristotle (384 BC - 322 BC), *Greek critic, philosopher*, physicist.

PART 2

1. Shirley Temple Black, born in 1928, is an American film and television actress. She started her film career at the age of three in 1932 and became an overnight sensation with her curly locks in her role in Bright Eyes (1934).

2. Mary Ann Halpin, *Fearless Women Fearless Wisdom*, Fearless Women Publishing, 2010, pg. 50.

3. Dr. John Gray, *Men are from Mars, Women are from Venus*, HarperCollins Publishers, May 1992.

4. T. Harv Eker, *The Secret Psychology of Wealth,* www.abundance-and-happiness.com/t-harv-eker-the-secret-psychology of Wealth.

5. Mother Teresa, *Nobel Lectures, Peace 1971-1980*, Editor-in-Charge Tore Frängsmyr, Editor Irwin Abrams, World Scientific Publishing Co., Singapore, 1997.

6. Gary Craig, *Emotional Freedom Technique (EFT)*, EFT Home - World Center for EFT - Emotional Freedom Technique www.emofree.com

7. Corrie Ten Boom was a Dutch Christian who with her father and other family members helped many Jews escape the Nazi Holocaust during World War II. She and her family were caught and sent to a concentration camp. Autobiography, The Hiding Place, Chosen Books, 1971.

8. Louise L. Hay, *Heal Your Body*, Hay House, Inc., Carson, CA 1984.

9. Joseph Pilates: Founder of the Pilates Method of Exercise, a Brief Biography of Joseph Pilates, Marguerite Ogle, September 2012. http://pilates.about.com/od/whatispilates/a/WhatIsPilates.htm Pilates is a physical fitness system that builds flexibility, muscle strength and endurance. It emphasis is on breathing, developing a strong core or center, improving coordination and balance and spinal and pelvic alignment.

10. John Maxwell, *Everyone Communicates Few Connect*, Thomas Nelson, 2010.

11. John Maxwell, *Encouragement Changes Everything*, Thomas Nelson, 2008.

12. *Life Application Study Bible, The New International Version*, Romans 12:2, Zondervan, 1991.

13. Deepak Chopra, the answers to our health and happiness can be found internally, *Chopra Center for Well Being*, La Jolla, California.

14. *The Bible in Today's English Version (TEV)*, Proverbs 4:23, published under license from Thomas Nelson Publishers, 1976.

15. Marianne Williamson, *A Return to Love: Reflections on the Principles of A Course in Miracles* (1992) Chapter 7, Section 3.

16. Wayne Dyer, *Excuses Begone! How to Change Lifelong, Self-Defeating Thinking Habits*, Hay House May 26, 2009

17. Shawn Achor, *The Happiness Advantage*, Crown Publishing Group, 2010.

18. Ann Geddes, Father's Day Quote, an Australian-born photographer, clothing designer and businesswoman who now lives and works in New Zealand. She is known for her stylized depictions of babies and motherhood.

19. Harriet Lerner, *The Dance of Anger*, William Morrow Paperbacks, 2005.

20. John Gray, *Men, Women and Relationships*, Beyond Words Publishing, Inc., 1990.

21. Ellen Bass and Laura Davis, *Courage to Heal, Harper Perennial, 3rd Edition Revised and Updated*, 1994.

22. Rick Warren, *Start the Healing by Revealing the Hurt*, Daily Hope Devotional - July 27, 2012.

23. Christiane Northrup, *Mother-Daughter Wisdom*, Bantam Books, 2005, p. 3.

24. Life Application Study Bible, New International Version (NIV), Matthew 7:7, Zondervan, 1991.

25. Oliver Wendell Holmes, Jr. was an American jurist noted for his long service, his concise and pithy opinions and his deference to the decisions of elected legislatures, he is one of the most widely cited United States Supreme Court justices in history, particularly for his "clear and present danger" majority opinion in the 1919 case of Schenck v. United States.

26. Mother Teresa, *Blessed Teresa of Calcutta*, born Agnes Gonxha Bojaxhiu and commonly known as Mother Teresa of Calcutta, was an Albanian-born Indian Roman Catholic nun. She was the recipient of the Nobel Peace Prize in 1979.

27. Oprah Winfrey, Oprah Winfrey Network (OWN), http://www.oprah.com/own

28. Rick Warren, Pastor of Saddleback Church.

29. *As Good As It Gets*, film with Jack Nicholson and Helen Hunt, You Tube, Best-of As Good as It Gets.

30. Corrie Ten Boom, *Tramp for the Lord*, 1974, she tells the story of an encounter while she was teaching in Germany in 1947. She was approached by a former Ravensbrück camp guard, one who had been most brutal and cruel. She was reluctant to forgive her, but prayed that she would be able to and she did.

31. Gavin De Becker, *The Gift of Fear*, Dell Publishing, 1997.

32. Dustin Rinebold, *Commercial and Corporate Pilot*, Interview, 2007.

PART 3

1. Andrew Newberg, M.D., *The Spiritual Brain: Science and Religious Experience*, Myrna Brind Center of Integrative Medicine at Thomas Jefferson University Hospital, University of Pennsylvania School of Medicine.

2. Wayne Dyer, *Excuses Begone! How to Change Lifelong, Self-Defeating Thinking Habits*, Hay House, May 26, 2009.

3. Dr. Robert Emmons, Thanks!: How the New Science of Gratitude can Make you Happier, Houghton, Mifflin Company, 2007.

4. Gary Craig, Emotional Freedom Technique (EFT), EFT Home - World Center for EFT - Emotional Freedom Technique www.emofree.com

5. Nick Ortner, *The Tapping Solution*, www.thetappingsolution.com/blog/tag/nick-ortner/ – Published, January 2012.

6. Deepak Chopra, Chopra Center for Well Being, La Jolla, CA.

7. Buddhist Proverb – It is only when we are open and receptive that we listen and learn.

8. Jonny Bowden, Ph.D., *The Art and Science of Coaching Weight Loss*, Intensive Training and Licensing Program, based on his best-selling product, Diet Boot Camp– ICF Certified Coach Training Alliance.

9. David Krueger, New Life Story® Wellness Coaches Training is a licensed certification program for professionals. This unique and effective system blends the insights of psychology, dynamic neuroscience, and the principles of strategic coaching.

10. Adelle Davis, *Let's Eat Right to Keep Fit*, Harcourt, Brace, Jovanovich; New American, 1970.

11. Pilates is a method of body conditioning developed in the early 20th century by Joseph Pilates and popular in Germany, the UK and the US.

12. HEALS – Health-Energy-Accountability-Lifestyle Shifts, Strategic coaching webinar series. www.leapheals.com, 2012.

13. T. Harv Eker, *The Secret Psychology of Wealth*, www.abundance-and-happiness.com

14. Chip and Dan Heath, *Switch, How to Change Things When Change is Hard*, Broadway Books, 2010.

15. Robert Maurer, Ph.D., *One Small Step Can Change Your Life*, the Kaizen Way, Workman Publishing, 2004.

16. Joel Osteen, Oprah's Life Class: How to Change Your Outlook Life Work - @OWNTV Oct 25, 2012 – As Pastor Joel Osteen says, "Whatever follows 'I am' is going to come looking for you."

17. Henry Cloud, Ph.D. & John Townsend, Ph.D., Boundaries: When to Say Yes and When to Say No, Zondervan, 2008.

18. Robert Harold Schuller is an American televangelist, motivational speaker, and author.

19. Trina Paulus, *Hope for the Flowers*, Paulist Press, 1972, page 75.

20. Jose Silva, '*The Silva Method*' considered the original and most imitated meditation program in the U.S, 'The Silva Life System' teaches students specialized guided imagery techniques to tap into their true potential and achieve their goals.

21. Oliver Wendell Holmes, Jr. was an American jurist noted for his long service, his concise and pithy opinions and his deference to the decisions of elected legislatures, he is one of the most widely cited United States Supreme Court justices in history.

22. Edmund Burke, was an Irish statesman, author, orator, political theorist and philosopher who, after moving to England, served for many years in the House of Commons of Great Britain as a member of the Whig party.

ACKNOWLEDGMENTS

First of all we want to thank the courageous women who dared to share their scars-to-stars stories openly and honestly in the hope they would inspire you to take bold action in your life. Even though some of them may have elected to change their names, to protect their relationships, the process of writing their stories, which brought up much of their negative pasts, was extremely challenging. We applaud them!

We are also grateful to the women who participated on the marketing research team for *RE*. They were willing to read through the manuscript and complete the exercises in order to give us their valuable feedback.

For all the graduates of our courses who have participated, staffed, supported, practiced, and initiated amazing changes and created phenomenal results in their own lives, thank you for your trust and appreciation of this dynamic personal-development work. Thank you to the Orange County, Pittsburgh, Boise, Ventura, and Sacramento women, who raised funds and volunteered their time to promote and staff our courses and who donated their time to CARTE's child abuse prevention programs. You are all loved and appreciated, and you have made a difference in the lives of so many families.

Thank you from Rose I thank my family and friends for being a part of my amazing network of support. I felt your love throughout my illness and recovery. A year later, I still catch my breath as I reminisce about the circumstances, my journey, and the countless blessings. I am so grateful for my son, Blaine, my family: Heather, Stuart, Char, Michael, Danny, my 88 year-old mother, Marjory, and my son's, dad, Dan. You sacrificed much and "caught me when I fell". I am thankful for my Orange County network of dear friends, including my prayer group and coworkers in Team Decision Making. You are too many to begin to name individually. I also want to extend my love and appreciation for my Pittsburgh family of friends, who were extraordinary under fire! You sent your love, prayers, and well wishes; and contributed funds and gifts during my recovery. In my absence, you supported, inspired, and empowered Gloria to continue the work for which we are both so dedicated. I am humbled and honored to call you torch bearers and treasured friends. And, Gloria, you had my back. You orchestrated "Project Recovery," opening your heart and home to worried family and friends; and you shouldered the weight of our course-work during my recovery. We have laughed, cried, designed, and facilitated courses together for over 20 years, and now, we have written a book together. Even through the editing, what a team we make, you and me! I thank you my friend. You have my heart.

Gratitude from Gloria I am thankful to my parents, Dan and Cecile, for leaving me such a powerful legacy of love and family. I am grateful and proud of my children, Larry and Renee and their spouses, Bonnie and Sean, for being such amazing human beings and loving parents. I want to acknowledge my three grandsons, Nate, Braeden, and Luke and my one granddaughter, Raegan, for showing me the true meaning of authentic and, most of all, I want you to know, I love being your G.G. (Grandma Gloria). I also love being "Auntie" to all my first and second generation nieces and nephews in California and Canada. I am also grateful for all the friendships that continue to inspire and encourage me. And, finally, thank you to Rose for coauthoring this book with me over the months of getting on "Go to Meeting" (at times between Switzerland, London, France, Germany, Sacramento, and Orange County, CA) and through all the edits, distractions, travel and work. You have been a true partner in excellence.

We want to thank Jeff and Aftan Murphy for their tireless enthusiasm and support. We are also grateful for Jeff's creativity in designing and getting our book ready for print. They both were our patient angels through all the changes and edits. Their company, Exclusive Image is one of the corporate sponsors and a STARR partner of our nonprofit, CARTE.

This book would have never materialized without the promotional knowledge, technology skills, and volunteer support of John Chapman and his company, Cybris. We depended on his expertise, counsel, and problem-solving abilities, on so many occasions, throughout this process. Cybris is also a corporate sponsor of CARTE.

AUTHORS' BIOS

Rosalie D. Gibbons has bachelor degrees in psychology and sociology and a master's degree in counseling psychology. She has been a licensed marriage, family therapist in the state of California for 30 years with an expertise in developmental psychology, child abuse, and experiential learning. Throughout her career, she has coached, supervised, and trained educators, community partners, students, and associates in the dynamics of abuse and use of simulation learning. For 23 years she has served as a board member and the program director of the non-profit organization, CARTE. In this capacity, she designs and facilitates personal and professional development courses for adults and teens. She is certified as a Color Code Interpersonal Skills Trainer and a Developmental Dimensions International Facilitator. For 16 years she has worked in various assignments for Orange County's Social Services Agency, where she is currently a supervisor and facilitator in Training and Career Development. She is the proud mother of a son with a successful military career.

Gloria Manchester, is President of Leadership Education Action Programs (LEAP) designing, marketing, coaching and facilitating its various personal and professional development programs. She has been a pioneer and bold leader in this arena for over 30 years. Gloria was certified several years ago as a life coach by Coach Training Alliance (CTACC) and is now an accredited International Coach Federation (ICF-ACC), a Color Code Interpersonal Skills Trainer, and an Emotional Intelligence (EI) and Nutritional Coach. She is a cofounder and President of the nonprofit CARTE. One of the many ways she has raised funds for CARTE's STARR Program for at-risk teens was by marketing a relationship seminar by Dr. John Gray, the best-selling author of *Men Are from Mars, Women Are from Venus*. Gloria is one of the women featured in the 2010 Mary Ann Halpin book *Fearless Women-Fearless Wisdom*. She has two grown married children who are both thriving in their respective professions, and she is the proud grandmother of three grandsons and one granddaughter.

Authors' Purpose and Mission Statement

Our inspiration in writing *RE* was borne out of our experiential work with women and teen girls. The scars-to-stars stories demonstrate how any woman, out of her willingness to shift and the courage to take positive action, can re-story and renew her life. Our mission in expanding this work through this book is to provide you, the reader, the same opportunity.